# The Clock of Life is Wound but Once

## Essays and Anecdotes of a Globetrotter

Bart Scalzi

ISBN: 978-1-7166-9957-3 (sc)
ISBN: 978-1-7166-9955-9 (e)

Library of Congress Control Number: 2020914609

Illustrated by Bart Scalzi

Scripture taken from the King James Version of the Bible.

Lulu Publishing Services rev. date: 08/31/2020

*To you...*

*My beloved parents who departed on that journey for which there is but a one-way ticket, I dedicate these pages.*

*You traveled to this blessed land seeking a better life and, indeed, made your way admirably with courage, sacrifice, humble dignity and with boundless devotion and dedication to your family.*

*As I pen these lines, a tear appears, but I am comforted in That, one day, I know you will be waiting for me when I arrive at that final station.*

# Contents

# Preface

Now, how do I qualify to write a book on travel? Borrowing a line from the 19th century English poet Elizabeth Barrett Browning, I respond, "Let me count the ways."

From a lifelong love of world travel, there emerged the inspiration to pen these pages and to share with others something of my good fortune of having experienced a rich and exciting life of globe-trotting. I draw from this treasure chest of learning, discovery, adventure, and just plain fun to present this personal memento - a travel book, but one like no other. You will find a collection of essays and anecdotes that weave together elements of my personal life and the experiences of many years of savoring this diverse and wondrous world. I have chosen to spare the reader the routine run-of-the-mill travel book with its pages of information, recommendations and commentary on accommodations, restaurants, and tourist sights and sites to visit. What I offer here may be called an *anecdotal autobio-travelogue.*

Have you ever seen God? Well, I have - in the kingdom of Nepal, high in the lofty Himalayas ....and *she* was a sight to behold! Why, I have run with the bulls in Pamplona, Spain - four times! I guess I was trying to get it right and I almost got killed doing it! Talk to a living saint lately? I have, in the midst of suffering humanity and the squalor of Calcutta, India. The mountain mudslide in Venezuela nearly ended my travel days and it was so with that harrowing incident in Australia, which did not earn me a feather in my cap - more like a crack in my cranium. I have traveled with a burning spirit of curiosity and adventure, registering what seems like a million miles, "rounding" the four corners of the earth, and wandering across six continents, with only Antarctica remaining on my to-do list. Other than that, I must confess that I have not been to...Disneyland.

Perhaps I might inspire a love of travel in those now turning these pages. To the young I say, do as I have done and plunge in with both feet; do it, try it, savor it all, but travel with an open heart and mind. You will find yourself in a classroom like no other, supplementing, enriching, and vitalizing what you studied in your history and geography books and drawn from your literature or foreign language class. My words for the older reader are simple, indeed: It's not over yet! No reason to store your travel bag in the attic or let your passport expire. Dear readers, young and old and in-between, I leave you with these thoughts:

> The clock of life is wound but once
> And no man has the power
> To tell just when the hands will stop,
> At late or early hour.
>
> Now is the only time you own.
> Live, love, toil with a will!
> Place no faith in time, my friend,
> For the clock may soon be still.

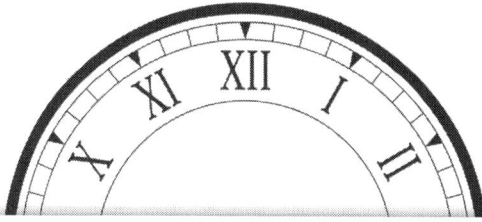

# Fiat Lux!

And the Lord said, "Let there be light!"
*-Genesis (1:3)*

Home Street...10 Home Street, to be exact. There, in a remote corner of White Plains, New York in the year 1939, I begin my story. Oh, that was not the year of my birth; that event took place ln 1933 and the family was then living on Brookfield Street. I was a child of six when the full light of awareness and recollection first flickered and established itself.

In 1932, Vincenzo and Elena Scalzi, with four-year-old Luigi in tow, immigrated to this promised land from southern Italy. My father went on to work as a groundskeeper for the Westchester County Parkway while my mother, with limited resources, managed to keep a loving, closely-knit home for a growing family. I was the first born in the New World, followed by twin brothers Mario and Vincent in 1934, while sister Mary was still in the planning stage and was not to make her appearance until 1941.

*Welcome!*

Home Street was little more than a worn patch of broken road that sloped down from Fisher Avenue on one side and up to Westmoreland Avenue on the other. When it rained heavily, the low center of the street formed a knee-deep pond and several cellars flooded. We kids delighted in splashing about, floating on rubber inner tubes, and courting a multitude of germs and illnesses. There stood a cluster of humble homes, Sheffield's Milk Company, Maccarelli's lumberyard, and an old mechanic shop.

Westmoreland Avenue housed the Cushman Baking Company which was occasionally visited by some of the local street kids in search of a delicious handout - by hook or by crook. One October day, big brother Lou and his buddies headed for Cushman's to raid the cake and chocolate trays in the delivery trucks lined up along the loading platforms. He came home with a Halloween cake that was a luscious sight to behold! The frosting displayed the colors of autumn, and the cake itself was stuffed with tiny trinkets. Of course, Mom questioned him about the origin of the cake, but he succeeded in convincing her that one of the bakery workers had generously given each of the boys some free goodies. That evening we happily enjoyed a rare treat, thanks to Lou...the thief.

Fisher Avenue, the other "boundary" for Home Street, was where we bought groceries at Seaman's store. In the opposite direction stood Rochambeau Elementary School, the scene of a personally traumatic event. Mom uprooted me from the coziness, familiarity and security of my home and deposited me in a room cluttered with tables, chairs, and toys and populated with children I did not know. After speaking with a lady seated at a desk, Mom kissed me and left; Oh, God, she *left* me! I ran to the window, climbed onto a ledge and cried hysterically as I watched my mother wave to me, smile and walk away. Hello, kindergarten.

The neighborhood was a veritable minestrone of Italian, Irish and German families scattered about. The "English lady" lived below us in our small brick tenement building and the Scatalone and DeMarte families occupied the floor above us. The Shays, with their own set of twins, shared our floor. Next door, in a little bungalow, lived a Black family, the Jeffersons, and behind our building were the O'Shays, living in a crumbling hovel. Mom would comment on poor Mrs, O'Shay and her struggle to raise five boys and cope with her heavy-drinking man. It was said that he drank heavily because he suffered from the effects of the poison gas that was used during The Great War of 1914-1918.

While our parents worked hard to maintain a decent home and provide us with our daily needs, we children could not be happier. Our concerns were few. The familiar jingling of bells signaled the approach of The Bungalow Bar, bearer of wondrous ice cream treats. We gathered about the vehicle with coins in hand and watched the man perform his magic, bringing forth cones and sandwiches and ice cream-on-the-stick. My favorite was the ice cream covered with shredded coconut. Often, on a Sunday, Mom and Pop packed a lunch, gathered the family and led us across the tracks near Westmoreland Avenue, escaping into the greenery and fresh air of the Westchester County Parkway. While our parents relaxed on the grass, we youngsters romped about, exploring the interior of the White Bridge or sliding down "Slippery Rock". Several times, while crossing the railroad tracks, I entertained a thought regarding the long tracks which narrowed and eventually vanished into the horizon. To where did they lead? What was there beyond that horizon?

Going to the movies was an infrequent but special treat and we were taken to the Keith Albee or Loew State theaters on Main Street to see *Tarzan of the apes* or that Western star Buck Jones; we laughed at the antics of Charlie Chaplin or Oliver Hardy and Stan Laurel. The evenings were for huddling around the radio, to be thrilled by *Gangbusters, The Shadow* and *The Lone Ranger,* to be scared silly by *Inner Sanctum* and amused by the shenanigans of *Duffy's Tavern* and *Fibber Magee and Molly.* Silly now, but one day my curiosity moved me to explore and find out from where those voices and that music were coming. I turned to the open back of the radio, searched through a forest of bulbs and wires and spotted a small, open space. Surely, this had to be the little stage, but where were the little people who performed for us? There were, too, the marvelous comics and some of our favorites were *Gasoline Alley, Smokey Stover, The Captain and the Kids, Flash Gordon, Dick Tracy* and the long-running *Mutt and Jeff.*

Often around home, I heard the names Vittorina, Zio Ludovigo, Antonio, Caterina and others. Who were these people? Why did they never come to see us? Where was *Italia,* so frequently mentioned at the kitchen table? One day, one of those dreaded black-bordered envelopes arrived and the scene that followed has never left my memory. My poor mother read the letter and then threw herself onto the bed and sobbed so painfully. Pop was at work and brother Lou was out on the streets with his friends, leaving us three little ones huddled around the bed, saddened, frightened, and bewildered. Her father had passed away in far-off Italy. Her father? Our Mom had a father? Perhaps a mother, as well? Why was she not here to comfort her?

The year 1940 marked a migration for the Scalzi family when we left Home Street, crossed Main Street and settled at 50 Ridge Street. It was a cozy little "Italian neighborhood" with a grocery store next door and the Assumption Church around the corner and up the hill. It was a year when the clouds of war had gathered over Europe and there was talk of someone called Adolph Hitler. That was far from our little nook of a neighborhood where peace and tranquility reigned. The only Adolph we knew of or cared about was Dolph Camilli, great first baseman for the old Brooklyn Dodgers. Franklin Roosevelt was our president, Joe Louis reigned as heavyweight boxing champion, and the New York Yankees ruled the roost in baseball. For the Scalzi kids it was growing-up time.

One day, Mario, Vincent and I discovered the power of a "magic notebook" in the possession of our mom. She often sent us to Saverio's next door to pick up some needed groceries. It was so easy; the man wrote something in the notebook and we went out with a bag of pasta, eggs and bread. We youngsters got the idea that we could have ourselves a grand party. We didn't know how it all worked, but it worked...until the end of the week when Mom went to settle the bill and discovered such items as candy bars, soda, packaged cupcakes, and ice cream. The party was over!

It was in that year and from that neighborhood that I launched my travel career: a daring journey of about eighteen miles, from White Plains to Camp Kitchawan at Croton Point on the scenic Hudson River. Mr. Tiano supervised and directed activities for a boy's club on Ridge Street called the Y-Rangers. Each summer, groups of youngsters were sent to the camp for a few weeks of swimming, hiking, campfire storytelling, Indian lore and exposure to nature's wonders. Brother Lou was already at camp and had taken our sole shabby suitcase so that when the bus deposited me at the camp, I carried my earthly possessions in a cardboard box. My first adventure away was an eye-opener: gatherings of bubbly young people, bunkbeds, chirping crickets at night. The food was strange and smelled awful, especially the boiled carrots and the creamed chicken. Where were the pasta and meatballs?

The door was opening and the path that I would choose to take lay just ahead. I was soon to leave the cozy realm of childhood and cautiously take that first step onto the world stage.

*Kindergarten - The start of a journey.*

# My kingdom for a...bed!

A horse! A horse!
My kingdom for a horse!
-William Shakespeare (1564-1616)
*Richard III* (with my apologies)

*Yeah...Bedbugs & Breakfast!*

There was an earlier time when it was my practice to arrive at a destination without a room reservation; I simply got off the train or plane and plunged into a city, sometimes at ungodly hours, and began the search for accommodations. Of course, there were often dire consequences to pay.

Throughout the years, I have managed to keep personal travel journals in which are recorded my daily experiences, impressions, and thoughts, with particular pages set aside for addresses, money spent, notes on my weight and fitness program and general travel information. One page carries the title "Superlatives" and registers the most, best, worst, costliest, cheapest, of everything I experience during a trip. My journal for the summer of 1978 reported that the costliest hotel was The Asbury in London, the cheapest was the Cernia Hotel in Belgrade, the best weather - in Paris. The dubious honor for positively, absolutely, the worst hotel of that summer (or ever) went to a ghastly unnamed hovel in New Delhi, India.

My introduction to India was not a pretty one. A new traveler there must first get past the initial uncomfortable reality of poverty and the crowded masses of a big city. It is a marvelous land of contrasts, a phenomenal history, fascinating culture and customs, but I got off on the wrong foot, to say the least. My plane landed at a late hour in a strange land of punishing heat and humidity...and a heavy, pounding rainfall.

At first, I considered inquiring about an escape flight out, but it was too late for that and I resigned myself to an unknown fate. I boarded an old bus heading for (I hoped) the city center. A huge flying insect rode into town with me and behaved badly throughout the journey, buzzing about, crashing into the windows - and my skull! The broken jalopy bus struggled through flooded streets and murky neighborhoods and into "town". I tried to communicate with the driver to make him understand that I wanted to get off at a place where I would have some hope of finding a hotel. I cannot imagine what I had communicated, but we soon came to a stop and I was deposited in only God knows where. The downpour had ended, but I found myself standing in a dark, soggy neighborhood of dilapidated buildings and muddy, puddled streets. I plodded through the swamp hoping desperately to find refuge. How did I get into this predicament? Of course, I fully understood the cause and effect of the dismal situation.

A dull light appeared at a second floor window of a nearby structure and it flickered "Hotel." At the top of the dirty, rotting stairway stood the – uh - *reception desk* behind which slumped the -er-*concierge*, a shirtless young fellow bathed in sweat, smoking a cigarette and listening to his small radio. Attitude? So indifferent was he that he would not have cared if Mahatma Gandhi had come through the door looking for a room. He pocketed my rupees and booked my room.

Oh, he booked a room for me, all right. He escorted me down the grim hallway to an opening in the wall that was meant to be my place of repose for the night. Passing through a dirty, hanging rag which served as the door, we entered my boudoir. My tired eyes opened widely as I surveyed my domain and looked upon, first of all, the frightful excuse for a bed. The lumpy mass that served as a mattress had a large yellowish-brown stain in the center and there was neither sheet nor pillow. But fatigue compelled me to accept my fate, for there was no place to which one could run. The small window had a ragged screen, but the mosquitos and crawling bugs were already inside with me. It was survival mode that kicked in and got me through the night...mare. That ugly stain might have been from vomit, bedwetting, or an oozing wound, so I spread a shirt across the blotch and lay down stiffly flat on my back, not daring to move an inch to the right or to the left.

With eyes wide open and finding myself trapped in an atmosphere of sweat, stench, and the miserably wailing music coming from the reception radio, I began counting the minutes and hours until my morning escape. Not over yet. Two lizards were positioned on the wall near the ceiling! I pondered how I could dare sleep and risk having a lizard crawl up my nose. Somehow, I endured until the deliverance of dawn when I hurried out the door with bag-in-hand and two under my eyes.

Linda and I shared an enjoyable visit to Ireland with our good friends Patty and Butch, doing a clock-wise circuit of that charming little isle, beginning in Dublin and making stops in Waterford, Cork, The Dingle Peninsula, The Cliffs of Mohar and Galway. We needed accommodations for one night in Cork and stumbled upon a B & B called Hayden's Place. It was a rather "informal" establishment with Spartan (and shabby) furnishings and decor. The towels on the rack hadn't been changed since The Irish Rebellion of 1916! Hayden himself, attired in a sweaty undershirt and rumpled shorts, served us...um...er..."breakfast". Our conversation at the breakfast table turned to how we had passed the night. When Linda and I complained of the cigarette burn we found on the bedsheet, Patty sat up and blurted out, "You had sheets?"

The Xiang Gang Hotel was tucked away in a nondescript Beijing neighborhood where I was fortunate to stumble into a reasonably clean and inexpensive room with a good breakfast included. During this stay, however, there were additional, unexpected amenities for the weary traveler.

My quiet evening sprawled on the bed studying my Chinese phrase book was interrupted by a ringing phone. It happened that a "friendly lady of the evening" was calling to offer her *special services* to me. How thoughtful! In my severely limited Mandarin Chinese, I tried to convey the message that I was not interested. *Bu yao* (Don't want), I responded. My guess was that I had not bu yao-ed her enough because I soon heard a knock at the door and in stepped the "friendly lady". When she realized that I was not a willing client, she asked for money for taxi fare. *Mei you qian* (I don't have money) and she departed into the night. Apparently, word had gotten around that a single, filthy-rich capitalist American was staying on the premises.

The silver jubilee of Queen Elizabeth's coronation was being celebrated throughout the United Kingdom, but it was not in my plans to join in the festivities - I had no bloody room. It was the summer of 1977 and London town was inundated by waves of tourists, which meant that hotels and B & Bs were fully booked. Some booking agencies were forced to send travelers out to small towns, often many miles from the city center.

Not expecting a royal courier to reach me with a special offer of a spare room at Buckingham Palace, I headed for Victoria Station where I found dozens of weary people settled down on the benches along the platforms. What to do but squeeze into a space on a crowded bench and attempt to snooze an hour or two. What did I care about Her Majesty's coronation - big deal! A brief period of semi-sleep passed when an ingenious idea came to me. I purchased return (round-trip) tickets to Gatwick Airport, about 40 miles from London center, and rode the train back and forth all night, managing to get some precious sleep time. God save the Queen!

My "boudoirs" around the world and down through the years have varied vastly, ranging from the cozy and charming to the creepy and revolting or, let's say, from a modest two-star hotel in Lisbon to a murky five-roach hotel in Bangkok. A few were nothing more than an uncomfortable evening on a park bench with the moon and stars as a roof. Somehow, such misadventures only emboldened me and I continued to challenge fate and take my chances. I could have made life so much easier for myself, but that was much too ordinary for my taste.

In the summer of 1984, I flew into Canton (Guangzhou) airport after a month of wandering the interior of China. It was already evening and my flight to Hong Kong awaited me the following morning. Of course, I did not have a room booked and arriving at a Chinese airport can be rather different from flying into Paris' DeGaulle Airport, London's Heathrow or O'Hare in Chicago. The facilities, amenities, rules and regulations often could be questionable, as I found out that evening.

The last shuttle bus into town had departed and the taxis had disappeared, as well. Not really a problem, I thought; I could settle into a seat in the airport and sleep a few hours until my early departure. Again, this was not DaVinci airport in Rome or Barajas in Madrid - Guangzhou Airport was shutting down for the night! At 11:00 the lights went out, the doors were closed, and everyone went home...that is, everyone but one soul - I had no home. I found myself standing alone in total darkness. Even the moon had gone home. I contemplated facing a long, muggy, bug-infested night.

When I spotted the lights of a small hotel at the far end of the airport, I made my way to the reception desk and inquired about a room. I was told that the hotel was fully booked, so I asked to spend the night on a chair in the lobby. The rules prohibited that, so I plunged back into the stifling unfriendly night. I stumbled about in the area in front of the airport building and eventually bumped into a structure with counters that probably served as a ticket center or a vendors' area during the day. I crawled onto a counter and, with my bag as a pillow, settled down for the night. Sleep was just impossible, lying on a hard metal surface in suffocating heat with those miserable bugs buzzing about my ears and vampire mosquitos sucking my blood. It all made for a memorable nightmare of an evening!

I tossed and turned and swatted the bugs and, with the passing hours, searched for signs of daybreak. It was so dark I could not see my watch and, except for the annoying sounds and bumps from the insect world, an eerie silence surrounded me in my outdoor hotel. Suddenly, I became aware of another presence – a form darker than the darkness - slowly moving towards me. When it lighted a cigarette, I saw what looked like a rifle with a bayonet and I realized that my night visitor was a soldier on duty as an airport security guard. In a totalitarian state such as China, that could spell serious trouble. I might have been taken for a foreign spy or saboteur lurking around the airport and up to no good. Now, that could have gotten me arrested...or even shot on the spot!

With the faceless figure standing silently before me, I scrambled to deal with my predicament and (I chuckle now) blurted out in my best Chinese, a cheery "Ni hao" (Hello). There was a pause and, without responding, he slowly turned and faded into the darkness of the night. Apparently, my limited Mandarin was good enough for him. Greatly relieved, I settled back and watched the dawn slowly unfold as my airport tomb gradually morphed into a real world of cabs and travelers arriving for their flights. I boarded my own seven o'clock flight to Hong Kong and got the Hell out of there!

Mother Nature, in its fickle and unpredictable way, can often thwart a long-anticipated journey. It was a stormy day coming down from Poughkeepsie and over to Kennedy Airport, but I confidently assured myself that within a few hours I would be comfortably settled in my seat and flying out of the nasty weather and on to sunny Italy. Entering the airport, I noticed the crowds mingling and the counters beleaguered by anxious travelers. Flights had all been cancelled because of the heavy, unsafe weather conditions! It became immediately clear that I was not going anywhere that evening! Although my home and comfortable, warm bed were but 80 miles away, I resigned myself to the reality of spending the long night in Kennedy Airport! My waiting espresso coffee in Rome would have to wait a bit longer.

The airport and airlines sought to ease our misery by providing the hundreds of stranded passengers with blankets and leaving them to decide where to settle down and spend the long night hours that awaited us. People were strewn about throughout the halls and spaces, sleeping on counters, in seats and on the floors. I spotted a space in the middle of a group huddled on a floor at the TWA counter. They were a charming, welcoming lot and we passed some time chatting and joking about our plight. The lady that camped out beside me was from Brooklyn and quite friendly and talkative. When I mentioned that I was from Poughkeepsie and a teacher there, she sat up and told me that her nephew was a gym teacher there, as well! Later, back home, I couldn't wait to tell Frank that I had slept with his aunt!

Years later, I did, indeed, change my ways and turned to booking accommodations in advance or arranging a booking at tourist counters at airports and train stations upon arrival in a city. Certainly, when I began to include Linda in my travels, I could not subject her to the follies of my personal travel mode. In the meantime, I went on my merry nomadic way, rambling about and "building character".

Not to say that an organized, well-planned, trip does not ever go awry. On a couple occasions, I returned to stay at a cozy Beijing place called The Ningbo Hotel. Because I was a familiar face, I fancied myself a favorite son of the establishment. That was until Linda and I arrived one day, fully booked and ready to take possession of our room. No rooms available! Oddly, my name was not even in the register although I had reserved weeks before leaving the USA; I was even in possession of a faxed acknowledgement of the booking. They acted as if I were a total stranger, and stood there silently as I protested in my tortured Chinese. A manager appeared and called us aside to explain that a delegation of the Communist Party was in town for a conference. It was clear, pure and simple - we got bumped by the comrades.

We were feeling rather adventurous one springtime and signed up to spend a night with a poor Indian family on a small island on Lake Titicaca, bordering Peru and Bolivia. Our tourist dollar would supplement their meager income and we were fine with that. At a 12,500 feet elevation, Lake Titicaca is the highest navigable (large ships) lake in the world. A small boat transported us across the water, passing the incredible "floating islands", which were completely made of thick layers of the *tortora* reed and were inhabited by the pre-Incan Uros.

Our host was waiting at the small dock and escorted us, gasping for oxygen, up a steep hill to the house where we met la senora and four teen-age daughters. Our room in the shabby stone hovel was stark and furnished with a large crude bed, a broken chair, and...a chamber pot. There were no heat, no lights, and no running water. The primitive toilet was outside and not inviting on a bitter cold or stormy night. We prayed that "the call" would not come. With all these "amenities" we had no choice but to retire early for the night. The cold was bitter and necessitated our sleeping in full clothing, including coats, hats and gloves. It was impossible to move under the weight of layers of thick blankets. Unfortunately, "the call" summoned us on that frigid, drenching, pitch-black night. The discourse approximated this exchange: "I'm going to use the chamber pot. Don't you look!" Response: "Look at you? I can't even see you!" Next morning, we had "breakfast", thanked our hosts and fled across Lake Titicaca and back to town.

I have come to some conclusions regarding travel accommodations. First, I don't need a spacious, ornate (and costly) 5-star palace. A clean, friendly, smaller hotel or B & B is fine, provided that the B & B does not stand for breakfast and bedbugs. Secondly, make those room reservations and have a clean, comfortable room waiting upon arrival.

Of course. the ultimate accommodations are the ones I leave behind, those "same old four walls" and that boring daily routine that I escape when I fly off on a foreign adventure. After weeks of romping through Europe, cruising the Caribbean or hiking the Canadian Rockies, home is so deliciously appreciated. The shower spout needs adjusting, the grass needs cutting and a bill or two awaits me at the mailbox, but I am home. Until I venture forth again, I will enjoy family and friends, relax under my old, sanctuary maple tree, read a book sipping a little vino and schmooz with my dear cat, *Starvin' Marvin.* Oh, how sweet it is!

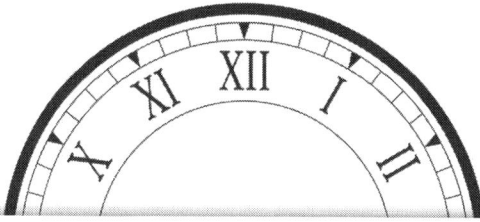

# Bon Appetit!

We should eat to live
and not live to eat.
-Moliere (1767-1825)

Sorry, no recipes here…and I won't fill these pages with recommendations for choice restaurants in Rome, Rio or Rwanda. Nor will I offer any suggestions as to where to soak up pleasant dining ambience. I leave that to the plentiful travel books available at Barnes & Noble and Amazon. I choose to only touch lightly and playfully on these topics.

Oh, I suppose I could provide a recipe or two if one were to insist upon it. Absolutely. Here is one I found on display in a history museum in Sydney, Australia and you can thank (or blame) a Peter Egerton Warbuten for this one. He was a 19th century pioneer at a time when the camel was introduced into the deserts and barren expanses of The Land Down Under. The rugged *prairie schooner* not only survived in the new world, but it is happily thriving to this day.

## Recipe for camel's feet

Cut the foot off at the hock and scrape and singe as much of the hair as time and appetite will allow. Stick the end in glowing coals, burn it for some considerable time. Then strike it smartly with a tomahawk. If charred, the sole will come off. Place the foot in a bucket and keep it steadily boiling for 36 hours. Then your teeth, if good, will enable you to masticate your long-delayed dinner.

And I can describe a culinary experience where atmosphere was everywhere to be absorbed. I entered a very crowded and noisy eating establishment on a bustling Hong Kong street. I settled at a rickety table where another diner, oblivious to the world around him, was ravenously devouring his meal. I attempted to eat my dinner in the presence of an uncouth, positively revolting slob of an eating machine with all the table manners of a Chinese dragon. This dining experience could best be described with five words: *slurp! grunt! burp! drool! gulp!* He added to the spectacle by occasionally cleaning an ear with his small finger, sucking his teeth and coughing across the table. He never once looked at me as he noisily chomped and munched his chicken and then spit the bones on the floor around us. Italy has its Isle of Capri and here was the Isle of Debris. I could endure this no longer, so I abandoned my plate and fled the premises into the fresh air, leaving behind a human disposal unit loudly slobbering through a seven-course orgy...and I do mean *coarse*! Traversing the globe and partaking of its vast and varied cuisines is an adventure itself. Every culture has its specialties and an open-minded diner should come equipped with curiosity and an iron stomach. A local specialty might be for you a personal disaster. I like to inquire as to the ingredients involved in that unrecognizable mass sitting on my plate. On the road, I do want to enjoy the local fare and not go looking for a hamburger joint. Certainly, my favorite cooking is Italian and in second place, Chinese. In fact, in just about every major city worldwide, one is likely to find an Italian and Chinese eating establishment.

When discussing the Italian table, two words come immediately to mind: pasta and vino, of course. Everyone loves a plate of pasta; and if you are curious about its history and traditions, there is a museum in Rome called The National Museum of Pasta. It is a unique little place.

After completing the usual tourist circuit of the Colosseum, Vatican, Spanish Steps and such, look for Piazza Scanderburg, near the Quirinale Palace and stop in for an enjoyable hour. There, one can learn about the methods and traditions of pasta production, the evolution of the machinery and tools of production and, also, view a display showing the many types and forms of pasta. Did you know that the names of different pastas are derived from their forms and shapes? Orzo is the Italian word for barley. Spaghetti is from the word *spago*, which means *string*. Penne means *pens* or *feathers* and Rotelle are *spirals*. Interestingly, the pasta we call "bowties" has the name *farfalle* in Italian and that means *butterflies*. Wheat products such as pasta were known in early times throughout the Mediterranean region. Marco Polo saw the Chinese rice equivalent and commented, "They look like what we have back home". The museum is The Louvre of Linguine, The Metropolitan Museum of Manicotti, The Guggenheim of Gnocchi,

Of course, a good glass of vino must accompany any self-respecting plate of pasta. I am not a connoisseur by any means and I don't know, nor care about anything as regards vintage or bouquet; I just drink it, red or white, always dry and with a meal or, perhaps, a bit of cheese. I do, however, know something about making wine - at home.

With the approach of the fall season, my father prepared for the annual ritual in the wine cellar. Money was often scarce, but he somehow managed to purchase crates of grapes shipped from sunny California and transported to local merchants via New York City. The whole family was recruited and dutifully employed in the crushing and squeezing of the grapes; the juices were then poured into three waiting barrels. Our equipment was rather antiquated, but my father the winemaker always produced a robust, rich red that would have pleased Bacchus, the Roman god of wine. Inevitably, a by-product of our industry and efforts was the squadrons of fruit flies that invaded the workplace.

When in Rome I always manage to make a stop at my favorite little hole in the wall for a good glass of wine and plenty of animated chatter. In fact, the name of the hangout is literally *Er Buchetto,* Roman dialect for "The little hole." It's near the Termini train station. There are four little tables, photos and mementos cover the walls, and a roasted pig carcass awaits in a glass case by the entrance. From that pig, stuffed with garlic and rosemary, are carved tasty slices of a Roman specialty called *Porchetta.* Alessandro is the personable *padrone* who runs a place which includes a colorful gaggle of vocal locals, and the occasional foreign visitor. On any given evening, "The Poet" might appear or Alfredo the old boxer, and "The Doctor." Bernard, a tall, former Swiss guard for the Pope, was a regular until his demise a few years back. A stop at Er Buchetto is good for the soul.

So, what's on the menu? In a Kunming eating establishment I had the good fortune of finding a menu in both Chinese and English and that was a good start until I ordered something called *Paper-wrapped chicken.* Now, I was travel-wise enough to know that Chinese cuisine offers many colorfully labeled specialties, such as *Thousand-year-old eggs, Bird's nest soup* or *Caterpillar fungus Duck (*No, really!) and I waited anxiously for my platter. It was a pancake-type wrap which was neatly folded over pieces of chicken and vegetables. Mid-way through the dinner, I spotted two young waitresses looking my way and giggling. I went on slicing and munching my meal until one of the young ladies approached my table and managed to explain to me that I was eating the wrap and that the wrap was, indeed, paper.

Linda and I experienced a memorable treat one Beijing evening. Returning from a full day of exploring, we wanted to have a hearty bowl of soup before going back to the hotel. The "chef" emerged from the kitchen with two heaping bowls of some sort of soup. A couple spoonsful and we had a name for that local specialty: Swamp Soup. Looking into the bowl I saw chicken feet, chicken heads, beaks, gristle and guts, all floating in the murky mess. I thought I saw an eyeball looking up at me from the mire. *Xiexie. Bu yao.* No, thanks.

The fish-fry that never happened was planned for a visit to a small village some miles out of Caracas, Venezuela. I had joined two local adventurers who were planning a jeep safari for the day. We came to a river where the local fish population consisted of only one species - the lovable, friendly and very hungry piranha. I learned that the fish was edible, and my companions came equipped for a couple hours of fishing. Our harvest was plentiful and we drove off to reach a locale where a friend would turn our catch into a tasty fish dinner for us. Waiting for the meal, an old man told us that the previous week there had been a festival with much food, drink and dancing. One gentleman, quite inebriated, attempted to cross a narrow foot bridge on his way home. He fell into the water and was disposed of by the fierce piranha. That evening we chose to go hungry.

So, what's on your menu? In 1990 I was spending a couple weeks in Chile and, in a restless mood, considered several possible adventures. An exciting visit to Antarctica was a consideration until I checked the prices and decided to postpone that dream for another year. Instead, I settled on crossing the Andes Mountains by bus and paying Argentina a courtesy call. The route we traveled was roughly the one taken by Jose San Martin, the courageous liberator of both Chile and Argentina. He made the crossing in 1817, hauling cannons and supplies over the rugged, mountainous terrain. An amazing feat!

On the other slope of the Andes there is the Argentine city of Mendoza. After dropping off my bag at the hotel, I headed for a restaurant in the main plaza. Now, Argentina is renown for the quality and quantity of its beef; after all, it is the land of the fabled *Gaucho* and *The Pampas*. What caught my eye on the menu was a tray of grilled meats, ranging from chops and steaks to ribs and sausages. Munching away at my delicious dinner, I came across a meat I could not identify, so I summoned the waiter who told me it was *ubre*. Never heard of it. The waiter then proceeded to use hand gestures and to pat his lower belly. When he took a napkin and drew what looked like a cow, I realized that I had been eating a cow's udder; not likely something that would be found on the menu at Burger King.

Ever wonder what goes on in the kitchen of your favorite restaurant? You might not want to know. In my Navy days, everyone understood that it was wise to maintain a good relationship with the cooks. My buddy Abad was assigned to the officers' messroom where several cooks prepared meals for the officers. Abad did not like lieutenant Kilshire who was, in fact, rather arrogant and disrespectful toward him. I stopped by the galley one Sunday morning to visit and chat with Abad. It was a hot and humid day when the lieutenant came down for a late breakfast, and he sat alone, reading the newspaper while Abad busied himself preparing his meal. The coffee was hot, the lemonade cold and the pancakes were stacked high. Before serving breakfast to his favorite officer, Abad took each pancake and, using it like a deodorant pad, patted it under his arm. Bon Appetit!

Any serious discussion about food and dining inevitably leads to talk of calories, girth and that rollercoaster of a ride that so many endure in life: the cursed diet. Those of us unfortunate enough to be passengers on that ride can attest to a personal, perpetual, up-and-down struggle to avoid looking like Porky Pig. The introduction pages of many of my travel journals are filled with pledges, promises and declarations to return from a trip in tip-top shape. "This is it!" declares one page. "I will do it this time!" or "It's now or never!" The sad truth is that I have succeeded many times and, understandably, failed many times! During my teaching years, I always returned from a full summer vacation of globetrotting, sun-tanned and as physically fit as a Roman god. My dear friend Helen, our teacher of German, circulated among our teachers taking bets that by December I would be back to my old misfit self. Inevitably, I failed, Helen prevailed.

There is another way of coping with the everyday, never-ending, frustrating dieting that plagues the American way of life. Try approaching it with plain old humor, even self-deprecating tidbits: I'm on a seafood diet. When I see food, I eat it. Perhaps, something like this: I'm a light eater. As soon as it's light, I start eating. Of course, the most important thing is to recognize and acknowledge that one, indeed, has a weight problem. You know it is time to go on a diet when you push away from the table and the table moves. It might be time for action when you look like you were poured into your clothes but forgot to say "when". Those who do not treat the topic lightly will acknowledge the fact that "obesity is widespread" and, indeed, that "a waist is a terrible thing to mind." Those of us who must count calories and deprive ourselves of the joy of good eating are deserving of compassion and understanding because "dieters live life in the…fasting lane." A closing message and warning for the incorrigible, out-of-control dynamic diner: Eat, drink and be merry for tomorrow you…*diet.*

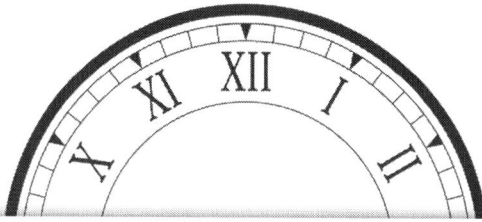

# Tower of Babble

I speak Spanish to God, Italian to women,
French to men and German to my horse.
- Charles V (1500-1558)

You speak a foreign language?

WOOF

Those with little interest in or no affinity for languages might choose to turn to another essay or watch a sit-com on television. As the French might say, *Chacun a son gout*......to each his own. For my part, language has been a passion, a journey of learning, stumbling. growing and of immense enjoyment and satisfaction.

Like so many millions of children of the immigrants that traveled to these shores from distant lands, we were bilinguals who spoke "American" at school, on the playground and at the corner store but, upon crossing the threshold of our homes, turned naturally and smoothly to speaking the language of our parents. My folks knew little English so that we children, although born here, spoke Italian first and then quickly acquired English as a second language.

There was also the phenomenon of developing a *mixture* of the two and creating a unique language non-existent outside of the family or our cultural neighborhood. All national groups coming to America experienced this. For example, Spanish speakers communicated in *Spanglish,* using peculiar combos such as *groceria* and *roofo.* Immigrants understandably struggled to assimilate and often found themselves applying Polish, Spanish, Greek endings and sounds to English words. My mother sent me to the *storo* to buy *miliko* and some *kendee* (candy) for me. She would say the sentence in Italian and incorporate these "Itanglish" words. Mike, my Polish-American brother-in-law, explained that his mother would come home with a shopping bag of milk, bread, butter and....... *grapeski.*

Along these lines, there was my special Itanglish moment when, as a young sailor first visiting our family in southern Italy, I faced the urgent need to "answer the call". While I could manage to communicate in the local Calabrian dialect of my parents, I inadvertently inserted some Itanglish, and that drew puzzled expressions. I asked to visit the *be-kow-so and n*o one comprehended. Finally, when I grimaced and rubbed my lower belly area, someone got it and led me to the *gabinetto* (or *cessu* in Calabrian) - the toilet...and just in time! Eventually, I figured it out. The early immigrants from Italy heard the word *backhouse* (outhouse) and did their best to approximate the English pronunciation, arriving at the word from Limbo - *bekowso.*

My father related an amusing story of his first visit to America. Like so many young men, he stayed in a boarding house where meals were provided at a community table. He was a newcomer with so much to absorb and digest about his adopted country. He noticed another boarder reading an Italian-language newspaper and inquired about purchasing one, as well. The other fellow explained where he needed to go and what words to say to the storekeeper. "Italian paper, please". My Pop repeated the words several times and, seemingly prepared, ventured out in search of the store. When he entered, he approached the clerk, braced himself and blurted out, "Talyen pepper, pleez.. The clerk could not understand his request. Again, "Talyen pepper, pleez". Nothing. Only God knows how this was delivered and how the clerk received it. Suddenly, the exasperated man came to life, turned to a shelf and reached for a package. Pop wondered about what he was handed but waited until he left the store and rounded the corner to examine this odd newspaper wrapped in a roll. Poor Pop...he had asked for the Italian paper and took home a roll of *toilet paper*!

When my mother arrived in America, her man had already been here four years "preparing the way" for her and their little boy. She faced a period of adjustment to the new culture and language, particularly when venturing forth to do some essential shopping, perhaps at Genung's popular department store. She surely marveled at the many cars, two movie houses, and numerous shops, everything so different from her quaint little mountain town of Cerva back in Italy. She quickly made note of something so confusing and strange to her that she could hardly wait to return home and question my father. When they gathered at the kitchen table for supper, she asked why Americans consumed so much salt. Of course, this drew a puzzled expression for a response. "Why do you say that?". My mother explained that everywhere she walked downtown, she saw signs with the word *SALE* - at shoe stores, pharmacies, hardware shops, markets. Pop must have been quite amused as he explained that the word meant *salt* in Italy (sah-leh) but something quite different in English.

Many years a teacher of Spanish in Poughkeepsie schools, I explained to my classes how my mother, too, had her coping moments with learning a new language. I related how she took one of my brothers to a doctor for the treatment of a toe infection. In her halting, limited English, she attempted to explain that her little son had a problem with his *feet fingers*. Both Italian and Spanish use "fingers of the feet" as opposed to our simple word "toe". She had understandably translated word-for-word from the Italian *dito del piede*.

The beginning of my fascination for languages can be traced to several phases of my early boyhood and this passion has remained with me to this day. My godfather, who lived upstairs at our 131 Cannon Street home in Poughkeepsie, read the Italian-language newspaper *Il Progresso Italo-Americano* and then passed it on to my father. At the tender age of twelve I was an avid boxing fan who scavenged anything in print about fights and fighters. I eventually had my turn at the *Progresso's* sports page and the boxing news within. It was all in Italian but my desire and hunger for the details of a bout or the background of a boxer drove me to learning and interpreting good Italian.

At fourteen I was going through a stage where I couldn't get enough of the American Indian, his culture and history, even to the extent that I could put together a full war bonnet using chicken feathers, and design and assemble a small teepee and moccasins. My involvement and fascination went beyond. I found a book in my school library which spelled out some phrases and vocabulary of the Sioux language and I devoured it all. I could now "speak" Sioux, although what I knew or could communicate would not have filled a peace pipe.

One evening long ago, my father and a few friends gathered at the kitchen table for a game of cards in an atmosphere of thick smoke, "wine-tasting" and lively Italian conversation. From my position on the floor where I amused myself playing with a toy, I frequently overheard the men mentioning my brother Louie and I could not understand why. Louie said this and Louie did that. Years later I learned that the name Louie sounded exactly like the Italian word *lui* which simply meant *him/he*. Those gentlemen were talking about Giuseppe or Pasquale or the boss, a neighbor, Mussolini, the pope, using the pronouns for *he* or *him* and not referring to my big brother Louie. An early seed of language awareness and curiosity was germinating within me.

There is a song from the Gilbert and Sullivan operetta *H.M.S. Pinafore* which cautions that "Things are seldom what they seem" and I can attest to the veracity of the statement. Driving down the mountainside one evening, returning to Barcelona with Anna Maria, Jordi and their two little sons, we were treated to a spectacle of lights bathing the city below. Our conversation was interrupted by the two young boys seated in the back seat who shouted a crude word in English. I was surprised and rather upset hearing such vulgarity from these two sweet, well-brought-up youngsters! "Anna, where did they learn such an awful English word?" After Anna peeled me off the roof of the car, she explained that I had heard the word "foc" which, in the Catalan language of the Barcelona region, simply meant *Fire* and, indeed, we could see a blaze at the city's edge..

That stroll down a street in Bucharest, Romania brought a smile to my face one sunny afternoon. The sign displayed on a shop window really caught my eye; I did a double -take. The sign announced in bold letters

*VINDEM CRAP!* Now, I realized that economically Romania was in shambles, but I had no idea matters were that bad! Anyone who has studied Latin or who is comfortable with a Romance language would easily see, for example, that the Italian *vendiamo* and the Spanish *vendemos* are related to *vendem* and they all mean *we sell*. Furthermore, the Romanian word *crap* is the English word *carp*. It was a fish market! Such a relief!

Each morning, leaving my hotel room and heading for the breakfast room, I greeted the staff at the reception counter with a cheery "Hi"- but this was Tokyo, Japan and that word sounds exactly like a Japanese word. No harm done, but now I realize that I was bouncing into the lobby every morning calling out. "Yes! Yes!".

Take the word *burro*. It is a simple enough word in both Italian and Spanish; they are pronounced exactly alike but carry entirely different meanings. After an extended stay in Italy, one could conceivably find himself ordering a meal in a Madrid restaurant and requesting extra *burro*, drawing a frown from the waiter. That request would be fine in Rome; it is Italian for butter, but *donkey meat* would not be on the menu anywhere in Spain.

Here we pause to address a pet peeve of mine. Do you enjoy the cuisine of Zhong Guo? Have you ever traveled to Suomi or seen a traditional folk dance in Magyar? Why, everyone enjoys Chinese food. A summer in Finland would be wonderful and a folk dance in Hungary is very colorful and exciting. The point: why, oh why do we need to rename, revise, distort, reshape the names of nations and cities around the world? We are perfectly capable of pronouncing reasonably well or, at least, of approximating the actual pronunciation of these places. In some languages, the capital of Russia is called Moscow, Mosca, Moscu. Children can easily learn to approximate the real pronunciation and say Moskvah. Do as the Romans do and call their city Roma and not Rome, Rym or Rom. It's Polska and not Poland or Polonia. Call It London and not Londres or Londra. Not difficult to say Nap-o-li for Naples. Japan? No, it's Nippon and Var-sahv-yah rather than Warsaw. How on earth did the Tuscan port city of Livorno come to be called *Leghorn?* Yes, Leghorn. Should, then, Polish school children "Polish-ize" our place names, as well? Would they be visiting our picturesque city of San Franciski?

How dull and ordinary would communication be without the colorful antics and games we play with languages in jokes, riddles, sayings, quotations or in an expletive or two. Caught once in a heavy downpour of rain, I found myself muttering, "It's raining cats and dogs". Later I got to thinking about how other cultures expressed this concept in their words. A Spaniard complains that 'It's *raining pots* "While in Italy you might hear *Piove a catinelle'*, a particularly imaginative expression describing a quantity of rain drops so dense that the drops appear to be millions of chains falling from the heavens. Relaxing in Hibiya Park in Tokyo I had a good chat with a gentleman about such expressions in the Japanese language. "It's raining mud and stones" I was informed. I also learned that while thirteen is a bad luck number in our country, for Japanese it is their number four because it resembles their word for *death* and is often avoided when numbering baseball shirts.

Early Christmas Eve in 1954 found me in New York City's bustling Grand Central Station, waiting for a train to take me home for our traditional warm and loving Christmas Eve celebration with the family. That meant so much to a young sailor far from home months at a time. Preparing to board the train for Poughkeepsie, I saw a weary traveler and a young girl seated on their luggage looking quite forlorn, tired and bewildered. Someone called out, "Does anyone speak Italian?" I answered the call and learned that the poor man was an Italian immigrant with his ten-year-old daughter, recently arrived and traveling on to Chicago. He was certainly in need of a friend. All their needs were duly addressed: the ticket to Chicago, money exchange, something to eat and, so important, enjoying some comforting communication in their own language. After seeing them off, I realized that it was very late and that I would miss Christmas Eve with the family. I took the after-midnight train home and did some reflecting on the journey along the Hudson River. It had been an unusual Christmas Eve, to say the least, but one of the most heartwarming ever.

When my father heard my tale, he smiled knowingly and nodded with approval and satisfaction. Then he related a story of his own. As a young immigrant, he settled in the city of White Plains. He spoke a fractured, almost incomprehensible English. One day, he took a local train to a nearby town and did not know where to get off nor how to make a connection. The train man did not understand him and was hardly patient, while seated passengers, some looking over their newspapers, offered no help. Pop was confused and worried until a black gentleman approached and managed to communicate with him and help him on his way. Years later he met the man on a city street and, recalling his act of kindness and brotherhood, embraced him and then took him to lunch. When the story ended, I realized the connection between my father's experience and that of the poor guy in Grand Central Station. That evening I slept peacefully.

To be sure, there is another dimension to the realm of human communication and it involves more than words, whether expressed vocally or in print. A hand gesture, a movement of the head or shoulder, an eye or eyebrow can say more than a thousand words, and the unquestionable masters of this "art form" are the Italians. I have observed two drivers passing each other in heavy Roman traffic and carrying on a lively conversation that displayed flailing hands, nods, bobbing heads and silent mouth movements that seemed to satisfy their immediate communication needs in the brief moment they had at their disposal. Amazing!

I was personally made aware of this silent language by my cousin Umberto in southern Italy. I had taken his two young children out to a gelateria for ice cream. Now, I pride myself in being a good speaker of Italian despite being American-born, so I was genuinely puzzled (and a bit annoyed) when the friendly ice cream man said to me, "You are American, aren't you?" Curses! How did he deduce that? I consulted with "Professor" Umberto who asked me to repeat exactly how I had ordered the three ice creams, "Tre gelati, per favore" I said in good, clear Italian. That was all! No, Umberto said, that was not all. He pointed out that, although I delivered the Italian well, I had accompanied my words with the gesture of three extended fingers and that it was not in the Italian way. Italians extend the thumb, index and middle digits. That was the giveaway.

I recall seeing a woman in silhouette on a balcony conversing with a neighbor and using both vocal and body language. A sight to behold, for she punctuated her words with hand gestures, flailing arms, a bobbing head and shoulder shrugs. It has been said that the best way to silence a talkative Italian is to tie his hands.

Then there are those occasional "incognito moments" that can provide amusement and a measure of satisfaction. One never knows what languages are shared with others around him. I had such a moment in the Grand Place square in Brussels where a crowd had gathered to enjoy a sunny afternoon concert and other entertainment. I noticed a couple that seemed uneasy standing next to a small group of lively young people from Morocco, I believe. They appeared quite relieved when the group moved on, but not for long. To see the performance better, I occupied that space and then heard the woman mutter to her husband, "Careful. There's another one of them." Now, in the summer months I do acquire a somewhat different aspect. The sun provides me with such a bronzing that, in my travels, I have been taken for Greek, Turk, Egyptian and Mid-Eastern. I turned to the woman and in friendly Queen's English, not Arabic, assured her, "No need to worry, lady. You are safe. I'm American."

I must say, I thoroughly enjoyed that incognito moment in old Napoli when, as a young sailor, I rode a city bus across town. Two locals sat behind me and diverted themselves by ridiculing me in Italian to the delight of several passengers. "Stupid-looking American" and "What a monkey suit". I sat through the show looking straight ahead until the bus arrived at my destination and I stood up, turned to my tormentors and said to them in clear Italian, "Is this the stop for Garibaldi Square?" That drew some laughter from several passengers as the two rogues sat mortified, and I stepped off with a cheery "Ciao".

At the start of every school year, I took pleasure in reading to my students of Spanish an article I had clipped from the New York Times. It was especially impressive for me, but I also thought it useful for my young people because it reinforced the idea that learning one language in the months ahead was not a monumental task. I read to them the story of a United Nations translator who spoke, amazingly, eighty different languages! Furthermore, he had not simply mastered the old standards - German, French and Spanish, but also such mind-scramblers as Quechua, Arabic, Welsh, Basque and Urdu! Astounding! Now, I never seriously aspired to becoming a true polyglot and dazzle the world, but I would at least have a grand time in my travels using English, Italian and Spanish, with a "smattering" of French and Chinese.

Happily, I have achieved my goal, although that "smattering" of Chinese once resulted in a Beijing taxi cab driver laughing so hard at something I had blundered in Chinese that he actually smacked his head with both hands and nearly ran us off the road! C'est la vie...I guess.

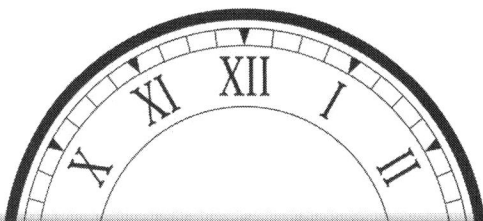

# Calabrian Roots

Fair Italy! Thou art the world,
The home of all art yields and
Nature can decree!
-Lord Byron (1788-1824)

Sometimes I think that God must be Italian! How else does one explain how this mere sliver of His earth has so disproportionately impacted the world, like no other in creation? It measures but a mere 116,330 square miles - about the size of California, and when compared to Russia, China or Brazil, it is but a plot of gloriously sunbathed terrain jutting out into the Mediterranean Sea. Oh, but what a plot!

Through the pages of recorded human history, Italy has been a cornucopia of beautiful art, music and literature, of inventors, explorers, scientists and warriors. Its cuisine is supreme and its people possessed of a warmth, charm, creativity and innate intelligence. Yes, Italy could qualify as a "chosen people". The Italian peninsula has nurtured lions such as Julius Caesar and Napoleon Bonaparte, emperor of France but of Italian blood. Giuseppe Garibaldi was the fierce warrior for Italy's independence and unity. Columbus, Verezzano, Cabot and Marco Polo were among the bravest of intrepid explorers. In an extraordinary manner, Italy has resoundingly graced, shaken and blessed world history.

USS Whitley sailed into the Bay of Naples in June of 1954. I was a young sailor of 21 years who was about to embark upon the wondrous adventure of a lifetime. The ship would remain in port for several days and that afforded me the chance of realizing a life-long dream. My childhood was filled with mention and talk of places and people in faraway Italy. So many names, but no faces except for those in worn and faded photos. This was the moment. I requested four days leave to visit my tribe in southern Italy and they were granted. I don't know how I managed to pull off this new and bold endeavor, but the dream was realized!

Calabria, the toe of the Italian boot, is one of 20 official administrative regions of Italy, along with, to name a few more familiar ones, Tuscany, Lombardy and Sicily. The regions are also traditional divisions with their customs, histories and some dialects so far from the official Italian that they require a special translation. For example, I am comfortable with the Calabrian dialect and could cope with hearing the Neapolitan and Roman dialects, while a few of those from the northern area belong to another planet. Historically, Italy has been divided in half: the South, from below Rome and the North, above. While the southern regions struggled with centuries of poverty and neglect, northern Italy flourished and maintained cultural and economic ties with other European nations. Fortunately, the Calabria I was visiting reflected a new awakening, more opportunity and a taste of prosperity.

Arriving by train in the city of Catanzaro, I inquired about finding a little town called Cerva, nestled somewhere in the nearby mountains. It was already dark, and a solitary taxi, fortunately, sat there awaiting a fare. The journey up the mountain was a precarious one because of the narrow, winding road and the steep drops along the way. The cab departed, leaving me standing alone on the street, in silence and beneath a bright moon. Except for a few dim, flickering lights in several houses, the town seemed asleep. I was pondering my next move when suddenly, out of the darkness, a loud cry, "Bartolo! Bartolo!" Cousin Vittorina ran toward me with open arms. One of the houses burst to life and people came pouring out to greet me. I shall never forget the moment. I was embraced and kissed by people I had never met! How did they know? I was told that my parents had written weeks before, explaining that their American Navy son might someday come to Italy and possibly visit them. The group had gathered for dinner when they heard the taxi, looked out and saw a uniformed young man. Bartolo, of course!

That evening I was centerstage in a room crowded with relatives and with more arriving. There were aunts and uncles and cousins chattering, emoting, and contributing heavily to my confusion and bewilderment. My Uncle Antonio playfully sat on my lap, asking me, "Guess who I am." while an aunt encouraged me to eat. Then, an elderly woman was ushered into the room; my grandmother and I embraced.

Cerva is a picturesque little village clinging to the side of a wooded mountain and seemingly isolated from the outside world, although Petrona', my father's birthplace, is about one mile down the road. The stone houses are clustered together, the streets are narrow and cobblestoned, with several public water fountains scattered about. There is, of course, the village church, where my parents were married in 1927. On that first visit to Cerva I asked to see the house where my mother was born in 1905. I was so moved that I knelt and kissed the stone steps at the entrance. The gesture, I later learned, caused quite a stir among the relatives and neighbors.

Of my four *nonni* in Cerva and Petrona', I came to know only my grandmother Saveria; the others were no longer in the picture. My grandfather and namesake Bartolo was the person for whom my mother cried so bitterly when that black-bordered letter arrived on Home Street in 1939 announcing his passing. Now I was left with the anecdotes and stories my aunts recounted about him. Nonno Bartolo was a hardworking family man, but also a festive sort who enjoyed his wine and good companionship.

He had visited America a couple years and returned with some dollars and a lot of broken-English expressions and comical melodies which he often belted out. He was known for not carrying a wallet and dropping money from his pockets. It was said that the village children often followed him to pick up any loose change he dropped along the way. Like my namesake, I have done the same over the years and my mother often reminded me of that.

In a rather bizarre and convoluted manner, I met my great grandmother Anna Rosa, as well- yes, my *great* grandmother. There was an anniversary of some sort and my Aunt Maria and I climbed the hill to the cemetery to leave flowers. At the family mausoleum she went about cleaning up and arranging, but occasionally explaining and describing the departed relatives who slept there. She pulled out a box that was under a shelf and sat down to rest and comment further. She began to stir the bones within the box and wistfully speak of this dear family member. "This is your great grandmother, Anna Rosa. I remember her as a sweet and loving person. Children loved her because she told them stories and always drew candy or chestnuts out of her apron pocket to give to them." She also explained that the bones were slated for burial elsewhere. Zia Maria was an original.

Cerva had character...and characters. Nicknames were quite common and often a necessity for identification and clarification. In a community over-run with Giuseppes and Marias, it was absolutely essential for distinguishing between Giuseppe the Fruit Vendor and Giuseppe the Cobbler or Maria the Giggler and Maria the Church Lady. I heard of a Serafina the Sinner and someone known as the Drooler. How these names were acquired is a comedic story in itself. I was told of one local who, as a young man, was counting potatoes and went on as follows: thirty eight, thirty nine, thirty *ten*. Yes, thirty ten. For the rest of his life he was known as Trenta Dieci. Another poor fellow was known to help around the house by washing the dishes and doing household chores. A no-no in a traditional male-dominated society. To the end of his days he carried the title Roberto the Whore.

There was the story of the village lady whose son was to perform in a play scheduled for the Easter Holy Week. The proud mother could not contain her pride and talked incessantly about her thespian son and his role in the upcoming play. If there were a Calabrian Academy Award, her son would win it, unquestionably. He was to play a Roman soldier at the trial of Jesus, and the mother broadcast it around the village. The play unfolded and moved to the scene where Jesus was interrogated, condemned, and then turned over to the soldier with the order "take him away." The guard stepped forward and responded with, "Tanto faro' (Will do so) and then left the stage with the prisoner. And that was all. Period! He would be known forevermore on the cobblestoned streets of Cerva as *Will Do so.*

I had the privilege of meeting Gypsy Mary, so-called because of her "original" clothing and hair style. She was quite elderly, but alive and well and living with her aged spouse in a small stone house down the road. Many years before, *Maria la Zinghera* was my father's girlfriend before he met my mother. He had gone to America in the1920s to work and earn some money for his return to Italy and marrying. Trouble began when he returned and, instead of going to see Gypsy Mary, paid a visit to a pretty young lady to whom he had been introduced and whose name was Elena Donato. She was to be my Mom. The little lady that stood before me was well into her nineties, but quite lucid and alert. I identified myself, we embraced and then she recounted, with an annoyed expression on her face, how my father had left her for another woman. Her good-natured husband smiled and told me that his wife still carried that grudge. It was gratifying to get a cup of coffee because I had envisioned being slammed with a frying pan and cast outside the door. I do wonder how my father and Gypsy Mary are dealing with the matter in Heaven.

Seated at the Dutch door entrance to his house, *Zio* Gabbriele could easily snare me as I passed his way. When the old gentleman invited me in, his wife Santuzza dutifully prepared the coffee and brought out the biscuits. Zio Gabbriele loved having me because I was the perfect listener and he the prolific storyteller. Because of his age, he could be forgiven a bit of boasting, exaggeration and embellishment when he weaved his stories of hunting feats and military exploits. He told me (not just once) how he had hunted and shot a large wolf that had frightened the villagers for some time. The animal was paraded through the streets with cheers and praise for the great hunter.

Most of his tales, however, were centered on his "extraordinary" military service in northern Italy during the Great War of 1914-1918. Important officers, he said, heaped praise upon him for his bravery, demeanor and general savvy. One day, while the elderly gent wove a tale of his glory days, Zia Maria came to the door calling me for dinner. At the table, I told my aunt of some of Zio Gabbriele's achievements and deeds in the war. Zia Maria, who never minced a solitary word, answered, "And did he tell you how he deserted the frontlines and fled to Cerva and hid with other deserters in the nearby hills?" They avoided the authorities by spending the duration of the war in the woods and having meals brought to them by their families. With those few blunt words, delivered by my Zia Maria, "General" Gabbriele Mazza was unceremoniously demoted to private!

Now, Cousin Luigi was in a category by himself in that he was a stellar example of what Italians call a *Menefreghista,* a non-conformist, a don't-give-a-damner. One day, I was treated to a story that could have been described as "survival of the fittest at the dinner table". The narrator of the tale was cousin Umberto, the scene was a local cantina in Cerva and the protagonist was cousin Luigi, an original, a classic, "a piece of work". Several friends had finished playing cards and were ready to share a delicious pasta dinner. When all were seated, a large platter of pasta and meat emerged from the kitchen and was placed in the center of the table. Luigi had a gargantuan appetite and when he saw the number of hungry diners at the table, he feared that he might be left with little or nothing. He stood up, reached over and pulled the platter toward himself. Then he deposited a generous wad of sputum in the center of the pasta and, oblivious to the loud chorus of howls and groans, ate his dinner. Yes, a piece of work.

Good Uncle Carmine took me to the village fair in neighboring Petrona' where I was first shown where my father was born and spent his childhood. Later, at the fair, I was introduced to an old friend of my parents, a kind and amiable gentleman. Growing up back home, I recall the occasional squabbles between husband and wife over the usual issues: finances, the children, and other misunderstandings. It was upsetting for us children, although their differences never amounted to anything and everything always ended well. However, I do recall a couple heated exchanges between the two when I heard my Mom exclaim angrily, "I rue the day I met Alfredo Scalese!"

Voila'!! Ecco! Behold! Many years later, Antonio Scalese and I embraced in a remote little town in the Calabrian hills. It was this same

Alfredo Scalese who long ago introduced my Mom to my Pop! He and I enjoyed a warm and pleasant exchange of questions and information, but I carefully avoided a detail or two. When we parted, I stopped short of saying, "Thank you, Alfredo Scalese, for first bringing my father and mother together. I am eternally grateful."

Italian politics can be described as one big minestrone. There was a time when a random gathering of twenty Italians was comprised of representatives of twenty different political parties. There were Christian Democrats, Communists, Socialists, Monarchists, Republicans, the members of which ranted and raved in praise and defense of their parties and the obliteration of all the others. The political landscape was strewn with the clutter of strikes, referendums, run-away partisan journalism, bickering and posturing among family members and friends. Several of us cousins had gathered on All Souls Day in the family mausoleum in the Cerva cemetery overlooking the town. It was a solemn moment of nostalgia and reflection. The five assembled cousins were made up of a Communist, a Socialist, a Christian Democrat, a Monarchist while I was the token Capitalist American. Cousin Umberto delivered a sobering thought as we stood where loved ones lay in eternal repose. "Let us remember that for all the political turmoil, wars, injustices and differences that exist in this world, we shall one day be as these loved ones here - forever equal." We crossed ourselves and departed.

Over the years, I have often returned to the little picture-postcard village cradled in the bosom of the Calabrian hills, and I have come to know and love it dearly although, with the passage of time and so many of its good people, it has been transformed. What was once a warm, pulsating and meaningful community of family and friends with its colorful traditions, customs and festivals, is now a veritable ghost town of old houses inhabited primarily by the elderly and those unable to migrate elsewhere. With the main players vanished, I see before me but an empty stage. Those early visits were like a stroll through an old family album where I filled in the faces and names of those loved ones I so often heard mentioned in my childhood.

How fortunate to have experienced the joy of discovering the ancestral tree and to have savored its precious fruit. I shall forever be grateful for the day in 1954 when USS Whitley sailed into the Bay of Naples.

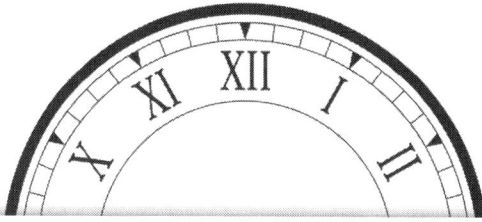

# Two paths

Freedom is God-given,
But often man-handled.
-Anonymous

*Twinkle twinkle, little star.....*

*Traiasca Partidul Comunist Roman!* proclaimed the billboards and banners of the city of Bucharest. *Long Live the Romanian Communist Party!* but millions of oppressed people held captive in their homeland did not embrace these foul words - certainly not Ortanza Gheorghiu. Romania had the misfortune of being, like Hungary, Poland and Czechoslovakia, another "worker's paradise" caught in that awful dragnet that was Soviet Communism.

When I first knocked, it was Ortanza who opened the door and provided entrance into the dismal life of her suffering land. The train made its way into Gare Nord railway station and to a new and sobering life experience. For some years I had sought to penetrate the Iron Curtain and visit the almost impenetrable Soviet Russia; Romania was to merely serve as a stepping stone. I am so happy that I made the stop, for unforgettable adventures awaited me and lasting, precious friendships would be forged.

The station was crowded and shabby and the sights, sounds, and smells around me indicated that a new experience was unfolding. I looked about and first noticed that I could manage much of the wording on signs and notices. Like Italian, Romanian belongs to the Romance family of languages along with French, Spanish, Portuguese and Catalan. The region had once been a province of the Roman empire and known as Dacia... but, I needed a place to stay and I headed for a small information counter in a corner of the platform. I joined other travelers waiting in line. The poorly-dressed people standing with me and seeking assistance spoke what sounded like Russian, Polish and Hungarian.

I finally stepped up to the counter and came face-to-face with a very attractive young lady...blond, green eyed and wearing a tired, unhappy expression on her lovely face. When she realized that I was not just one of the hordes of travelers from Eastern Europe but a Westerner, an American, her countenance noticeably brightened. She struggled to communicate with me in her halting English and we managed to hold a spirited conversation. Ortanza had a story to tell and she had certainly found in me a willing, attentive audience. She seemed to trust me from the beginning and poured forth her unhappy feelings about life in Romania and her deep resentment of Communism. However, we could not comfortably and freely speak in that setting, so I invited her to meet with me at a nearby cafe-looking establishment after finishing her day. We settled at a table in an isolated corner of the cafe and spent several hours conversing and getting acquainted with each other. We easily assumed our roles - she as my instructor and I as her willing, attentive student, anxiously hanging onto her every word. She launched into a narrative that was to serve me well in the following years that I would be visiting Romania and exploring the world of Communism in other Eastern European countries. It was obvious that she was an unhappy, suffering victim of oppression, but she was also an uncompromising, fearless fighter who would not go silently into the night.

She challenged and questioned her fate, despised the system and cursed her captors. Under her tutoring and nurturing I would come to see and feel and understand first-hand the true meaning of Communist tyranny. And I would come to know and admire Ortanza. She lived in a small apartment in one of those drab soviet-style, block buildings seen throughout Eastern Europe. She shared the home with her elderly mother and brother Niku, who was to one day escape to a free Australia. Ortanza contributed to their quite modest home economy by working as a tourist agent and translator at the railway station, but primarily at the main tourist bureau on Magheru Boulevard. She was poorly paid (as was everyone), but fortunate in that she worked in relative comfort and cleanliness. I had seen women laborers swinging pickaxes and hauling stones and cement on a street project during the night. There was, indeed, true equality in this Socialist paradise!

Ortanza was a very bright young woman; she once said that she possessed an electronic brain. Besides her native Romanian, she also managed a measure of Russian and French whereas for our communication, we developed a *mish-mash* of Romanian, Italian and English. We functioned adequately with this, although there were occasional amusing moments. For example, she confused and misused the words *kitchen* and *chicken*. "I cook some kitchen for you today" or "We go sit in the chicken." The Romanian giggles would ensue, accompanied by an American chuckle or two. On such occasions it was heartwarming to see the clouds of her sad countenance lifted and bright sunshine break through, albeit momentarily.

We managed to share a limited and controlled social life; this was not Paris, after all. An occasional stop at a restaurant meant meager menu selections and poor service. Television was ponderous with its continuous propaganda programs on the glories of Socialism. The supreme leader, Nicolae Ceausescu, was shown visiting happy and productive factories and farmlands, although the ordinary Romanian benefitted little from this show of progress. The state-run news presented the outside world as corrupt, exploited and unhappy. Whenever she saw scenes of Americans protesting the Viet Nam war, rioting and condemning their country, Ortanza was furious! "I wish these fools could change places with me!" The radio was as controlled and stifling, except for those citizens who secretly and daringly availed themselves of "Radio Free Europe". Everywhere there was an air of oppression, fear and deprivation.

Often, Ortanza and I visited Cismigiu Park where we could speak openly and she could vent her anger and unhappiness. One evening, we walked to a small outdoor movie that turned out to be a boring propaganda film. We decided to leave and made our way to the exit gate where a burly gatekeeper told us we could not leave until the movie was over. Ortanza angrily tangled with him in a heated war of words, but he remained ignorantly stubborn and kept his big arm in our way with his hand clamped on a crossbar. I grabbed his thumb and twisted it back while, simultaneously, Ortanza thrust her body against his log of an arm. We bolted and left Godzilla staring in disbelief as we hurried to the trolley before the police could be summoned. The company of a foreigner was a risky matter for a Romanian citizen. The authorities suspected Western spies or money changers and they surely did not relish the exchange of cultural and political ideas.

It was said that in any group of three or four, one could be a spy or informant, and people lived their lives accordingly. Ortanza and I devised a way of coping when in public. Strolling along Magheru Boulevard, we saw two men approaching from the opposite direction; she recognized one as a Securitate undercover agent. As they passed, Ortanza blurted out something in Romanian to me and I dutifully responded in the affirmative, "Da, Da."

While Ortanza was at work I passed the hours exploring the city and observing the inner workings of that corrupt and evil system. Occasionally, I stopped at the Carpati tourist office to bring Ortanza an ice cream. Seated at a park bench one afternoon reading my American newspaper, a man approached and sat beside me. A period of silence passed and then he greeted me in broken English. As in a movie, he looked about and nervously requested a favor of me. He had an uncle living in New York City and he wanted a letter delivered to him personally. Now, I knew the risks involved; the authorities usually opened and examined the contents of letters, looking for anything subversive. I did not know the contents, but he seemed desperate and I decided to take my chances at the airport security checkpoint upon departure. Fortunately, the authorities never noticed the letter and when I returned to USA, I completed my mission and delivered it.

On another occasion, my curiosity drew me into an Orthodox church where I found that a wedding was being performed. I sat respectfully and observed the rituals and ceremony with interest. At the conclusion of the ceremony, the bride and groom stood at the altar and received the good wishes of family and friends. What made me do it? What made me boldly enter the line of well-wishers? I kissed the bride's cheek and told her, in fractured Romanian, "I am an American friend." She smiled politely, but I could almost see a big question mark hovering over her head.

The summer of 1985 was to prove a turning point in the Romanian experience. Ortanza and I made daring plans to travel from the city for a weekend in the Black Sea resort towns of Eforie Nord and Costanta. She had never flown and the flight from Bucharest's Baneasa Airport was the promise of an exciting adventure and an escape from her drab and monotonous daily existence. Our troubles began when we approached the hotel reception desk to reserve accommodations for two nights. The woman at the desk was a rather brawny, severe-looking creature with stern, shifty eyes that moved suspiciously from Ortanza to me as she examined my passport. All seemed to be going reasonably well until she suddenly asked Ortanza for her passport. She had none to give and noticeably trembled as she presented her Romanian identification card. Not good. Romanians were severely forbidden from travelling with foreign nationals. Poor Ortanza feared that the SS lady at the desk was a spy and would report her to the authorities. As we climbed the stairs, I tried to reassure and comfort her, but no words seemed to ease her apprehension and fear.

The following day we visited a Mr. Dragomercscu, a friend of hers who was staying at a nearby hotel. The middle-aged gentleman sought to comfort her, too, as she expressed her concerns. They then turned to complaining about their plight under Communism, but carefully speaking in soft tones. The water in the kitchen sink was running full blast and I moved to turn it off. Mr. Dragomerescu gestured to stop and Ortanza explained to me that hotels were often bugged, wired for surveillance. The running water served to muffle and mask the sound of voices. I felt that I was playing a role in a mystery movie or spy thriller!

That evening at the hotel, Ortanza and I sat for dinner on the restaurant terrace overlooking the vast Black Sea. It was the perfect setting, under a bright moon and a canopy of stars; the lights of passing ships could be sighted in the distance, and two gypsy entertainers played their lively fiddles. "I know this system and how these people operate," she sobbed.

She was sure that the woman would report her to the police. The flight back to Bucharest was a long and somber one. She might have wished that the flight would somehow continue across the border into freedom. When I left Romania that summer, I did so with a heavy heart because I was returning to the fresh air of freedom and leaving behind an unhappy bird held captive in a not-so-gilded cage.

A year passed during which I received no word from Ortanza. It was puzzling to me because we normally several self-censured letters a year, letters carefully worded to avoid anything that could be construed as politically controversial. The answer to this puzzle would not come until the following summer, although I already harbored some suspicions and fears. When we met again and embraced warmly, I anxiously awaited answers and an explanation as to what had occurred during my absence. The account that unfolded was disturbing. That stern-faced woman at the hotel in Costanta had indeed reported her to the authorities! Ortanza was summoned to the police headquarters and interrogated intensely for several hours regarding her relationship with a foreigner, Bart Scalzi. She answered defiantly that, "I am a free woman and I have the right to be with my friend!" A bad choice of words and certainly the wrong attitude. When they realized that she would not be cooperative and could not be intimidated, they applied a different approach. They flattered her with compliments about her attractive appearance, her intelligence and even her spirited defense under pressure. She was then offered a special position as a translator-spy for the government. She refused angrily - and recklessly - with the words "I will not work with you Socialist pigs!"

They retaliated harshly. Ortanza was quickly removed from her comfortable position at the tourist office and "offered" a job as a ticket taker on a rickety, rumbling trolley on the all-night shift. She declined, defiantly. Subsequently, her home was subjected to disruptive searches by the authorities. She and her mother watched and wept as the brutes plundered the rooms, looking for any incriminating evidence, such as foreign currency, perhaps dollars from the American.

I decided then that I could no longer endanger and upset her already severely compromised life. She wept and pleaded, "You are my dear friend and must not leave me!". She explained that I was a welcome respite from her dismal existence. I never again returned to Ortanza in Romania.

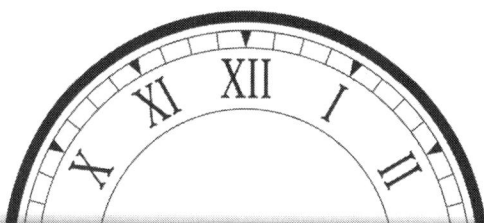

# And then there was...

Patience can be bitter,
but its fruit is sweet.
-Jean Jacques Rousseau (1712-1778)

And then there was Serban. I liked the guy from the first day we met. He was a personality package like few others I had ever encountered before in all my travels. Serban (pronounced *Sher-bahn)* was ever-smiling, enthusiastic, alert and the very personification of patience and practicality. His intelligence was quite impressive and it came with a genuinely disarming humility and humanity. In so many ways, he was the very opposite, the antithesis of his bitter, unhappy compatriot, Ortanza, especially in the paths that they had chosen for their struggle with the Socialist reality. This was Dr. Serban Nicolae Moldor.

We met purely by chance when I accompanied Ortanza to a local clinic for a sinus treatment by this doctor friend, an otolaryngologist (ear, nose, throat specialist). Serban put me at ease with his friendly and unassuming manner. We moved into a lively, spirited conversation on a variety of topics, especially regarding Romania's plight. Following her treatment, Serban and I agreed to meet the next day at a beer garden. He was to become my personal probe, my eyes and ears, my "undercover informant" in that Socialist paradise; I was his special link with the free world, and I believe we served each other well.

Serban spoke several languages besides his native Romanian. He was quite comfortable with German and Russian and I was already aware of his prowess in English. I asked him one day, "How do you explain your flawless, almost accent-free English language skills?" Typically, he simply explained that he watched a lot of foreign films and listened to Radio Free Europe, which was broadcast from the West and penetrated the Iron Curtain. Certainly, my friend was not oblivious to nor detached from the plight of his native land. He, too, existed under the yoke of Communist tyranny and had to endure deprivation and total submission. However, he knew how to survive, how to cope in the miserable world he shared with a suffering, simmering Ortanza Gheorghiu. "This evil cannot endure," he said to me. "The day will come when we shall breath the fresh air of freedom". Well said, dear friend.

Serban lived in a cramped apartment with his wife Adriana (also a surgeon) and two charming young daughters, Micaela and Ioana. Although he was a surgeon, he was poorly compensated and often brought home eggs and produce he received from his patients. Few cars circulated on the streets of Bucharest at the time, but Serban managed to purchase an old jalopy, a Czech Skoda, which he nursed and meticulously maintained because there was a scarcity of parts and services. He cleaned parts constantly and caressed every nut and bolt. When he needed to replace a car part he simply made it himself in a friend's shop or in a neighbor's cellar.

His parents, retired lawyers, were living in the city of Brasov, deep in the central region of Transylvania, about a two-hour drive from Bucharest. I shall forever cherish the memory of those two wonderful people! During that first visit and in several subsequent ones, I received much love, warmth and caring from them. They prepared sumptuous dinners of lamb, moussaka, sarmale which were accompanied by goblets of that Romanian plum brandy favorite, *tsuica*. Our cheery and lively conversation was frequently punctuated by tsuica toasts. Serban did a masterful job of translating for us, but we created a communication blend of Italian, Romanian and French that served us rather well. The tsuica helped, too.

In Bucharest one could enter an official government tourist shop where tourists could purchase perfumes, chocolates, cigarettes and more. That is, everyone was welcome except Romanians. The government badly needed the hard currencies of foreign countries in order to do business in world markets. They wanted German marks, French francs, British pounds and American dollars. The Romanian *Leu* was useless. Several times I did the Moldors a favor and shopped for them with my dollars. Such a happy household when I returned with the purchases! Of course, there was the element of risk, and fool-proof strategy was required. We devised a plan where I would exit the shop and walk several blocks to a designated spot where Serban waited in his car and we could drive away with the "loot." I was happy to do this for my friends. Serban himself needed foreign currency and worked out a deal where he and I both benefitted. He gave me a generous rate of exchange, explaining that he had plenty of *leu* because he could buy little or nothing in their meager economy. On the other hand, dollars would one day serve him well - someday.

An extraordinary experience was afforded me when Serban invited me to watch him perform an operation. I made my appearance at the main hospital at the appointed hour and Serban provided me with surgical gown, cap and gloves, transforming me into Dr. Scalzi. He led me into the operating room where an anesthetized patient lay on a table, prepared for a deviated septum procedure. He strongly advised me not to speak at all because his supervisor might stop in for a look and that could cause problems. I had the role of visiting American surgeon. Serban did his work, without an assistant to sop up the blood and hand him instruments. Of course, the supervisor entered the room and spoke with Serban about the surgery and then inquired about me. I basically understood Serban explaining in Romanian that I was a visiting American surgeon. To make things look more realistic, I quickly bent over the patient as if to examine the procedure more carefully. The supervisor nodded respectfully to us both and withdrew, leaving us much relieved. We survived and so, happily, did the bloody patient.

I got the brilliant idea of doing something special for my next visit to Romania. I did some grocery shopping in Rome and flew off to Bucharest carrying a package of pasta, a jar of good tomato sauce, a bottle of extra virgin olive oil, some grated Parmesan cheese and a bottle of Chianti wine. The garlic and basil would be available there. I wanted to prepare an Italian pasta dinner for Serban's parents in Brasov. Unfortunately, Serban and Adriana were on medical duty at the hospital and were not available for making that excursion. He encouraged me to make the journey anyway, assuring me that his folks were anxiously waiting for me and that I would enjoy the stay.

When I arrived at the Brasov train station, there was Domnul (Mister) Moldor with a big smile on his happy face and waving his hands. We drove home to their modest residence and to the welcoming arms of Serban's Mom. We went to work preparing our feast: while I boiled the water for the pasta and heated the sauce, Doamna (Mrs) prepared the meat and fixed a salad. I later learned from Serban that his father had scoured the neighborhood looking for a decent cut of steak and good bread. People owed him favors and he turned to them for help. The dinner table was a wonderful display of goodness! I repeat that we had no common language but functioned adequately with our mixture of Romanian, Italian and French. Our speaking skills improved noticeably with each glass of wine and tsuica. Domnul Moldor unloaded a hundred toasts in Italian, each delivered with a hearty laugh. "Salute!" he called out repeatedly and I echoed it in kind. He had picked up some words visiting Italy before the war. God only knows how we did it, but we conversed for hours on politics, Communism, travel and life overall. A wonderful time! At bedtime, Doamna Moldor adjusted my bed, tucked me in (yes, tucked me in!) and kissed me "Bon nuit". She fell short of singing me a lullaby, God bless her.

One summer, Domnul Moldor humbly requested a favor of me and I was so happy to be asked. Before the war and the Communist takeover of Romania, he spent some time visiting Italy where he became acquainted with the famous Borsalino hat. He asked me, if possible, to purchase a hat for him and that he would gratefully and generously compensate me. I would not accept payment, but I was quite pleased to be able to help him. I made the purchase when I flew back to Rome and I mailed it to him. The following year I returned to Romania and with Serban and family visited the Moldors in Brasov. We were socializing in the parlor when Domnul Moldor left the room for a moment. When he returned, not only was he proudly wearing his classy Borsalino, but also a glorious smile on his face! He wanted to pay me but that, of course, was out of the question. He explained, however, that the postal ignoramuses had opened the package, summoned him and told him to surrender the hat or pay a heavy fine to keep it. The dear guy assured me that it was worth every leu to be able to have his Borsalino.

Serban and I shared many pleasant moments seated in a beer garden, strolling in town and occasionally relaxing at his home in the company of his fine family. Adriana carried a sad expression on her face and brooded somewhat, much like Ortanza. Serban, of course, remained a beacon of cheerfulness in the house, while the children were children and not really feeling nor understanding the full impact of the politics and economy under Communist rule. I wished so much that they would one day live in freedom and true happiness.

Serban was invited to a private house party and he wanted me to come along to share a social evening with his friends. I welcomed it, for this was an opportunity for me to see another aspect of life under totalitarianism. I was introduced to a gathering of intellectuals and professionals including engineers, professors, an author and a poet. It was a varied group indeed but all of the same thinking regarding their contempt for and opposition to a Communist Romania and Communism everywhere. The evening was alive with conversation, political commentary and laughter. Serban most thoughtfully translated much of the activity and many hilarious jokes ridiculing the Socialist reality. One fellow mocked the state-run propaganda news system by jokingly delivering this one: "New York: riots in the streets...Washington: corrupt politician arrested...San Francisco: anti-Viet-Nam protests...St. Louis: increased violent crime...Denver: terrible earthquake...and Bucharest: The daffodils in Cismigiu Park are in full bloom this Spring". The group closed the evening with batteries recharged, their spirits replenished and better able to face the drab lives and routine that awaited them the following day.

Serban Nicolae Moldor. He brought sincerity, warmth and caring to our friendship. He afforded me a unique and intelligent insight into the workings of a "worker's paradise". He was aware of the rules and limitations, but he knew how to work safely around them. On the surface he was the model subdued Romanian citizen, working, raising his family and resigned to his fate. He did not "rock the boat" and become the object of the unwanted attention of the authorities as had done our Ortanza. He was patiently planning; he was calculating; Serban was biding his time.

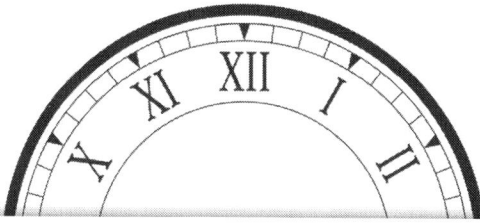

# A Musical Diary

Life is a symphony of the senses.
-Anonymous

Seriously, I once considered composing an original musical work...an opera, a hymn or a popular tune that would hit the charts with great acclaim. However, a sobering realization came to me one day - I could not read music and I was not able to distinguish between a written note of music and an ink blot. I decided to humbly take a seat with the listening audience and that was that!

Ah, but it did not end there. I convinced myself that I was indeed capable of a musical composition, of a sort. It was clearly within my grasp, I told myself, because unwittingly, I had been assembling it a lifetime. All that was required of me was my memory, nostalgia… and some plagiarizing of the musical works of others. Unlike the cold printed word of the traditional personal diary or autobiography, this is an arrangement, a stringing together of the songs and melodies that have marked the meaningful moments, events and people throughout the years.

A majestic rendition of "Pomp and Circumstance" will stir within me the emotions and nostalgia of graduation day, leaving friends and innocent school days behind and venturing forth into a new world. "Anchors Aweigh" brings back memories of those carefree days of youth and Navy days of adventure, comradery and the discovery of faraway lands.

The music diary may draw from the recollections of an early lullaby, that first girlfriend, a wedding, the loss of a family member or friend. I can drift back to kindergarten days when we sang a tune called "The Muffin Man" and another, "Pop goes the weasel." A popular song on the radio then was "Jeepers Creepers" which takes me back to that long-ago Home Street neighborhood in White Plains. In 1940, people were listening to and singing the lovely melody "Maria Elena" and the galloping nonsense tune "Hutsut Ralston."

With the outbreak of World War II, there was no scarcity of songs, ranging from the patriotic and sentimental to the silly and free-wheeling fun tunes. In elementary school at old Columbus School in Poughkeepsie, we sang, among other tunes, a patriotic "Let's remember Pearl Harbor" right there in class. Another was "She's a grand old flag." The radio supplied us with "Right in the Fuhrer's face" and "Coming in on a wing and a prayer." I was so touched by "The White Cliffs of Dover" and "When the lights go on again all over the world", both expressing the yearning for hope and peace for a war-weary world. The words and sentiments of such melodies really said it all.

There'll be bluebirds over the White Cliffs of Dover,
Tomorrow, just you wait and see.
There'll be love and laughter and peace ever after,
Tomorrow, when the world is free.

The shepherd will tend his sheep, the valley will bloom again,
And Johnny will go to sleep in his own little room again.
There'll be bluebirds over the White Cliffs of Dover
Tomorrow, just you wait and see

But, we youngsters, mercifully, had the distractions of childhood that made life almost normal for us. We went to school, played in the streets and, of course, read the comics and listened to the radio.

As the war raged in Europe and the Pacific, many communities took special measures for the defense and security of its citizens. I vividly recall the "blackouts". The chance of a night aerial attack by Nazi bombers was remote, but nevertheless a possibility, so the cities, towns and countryside were ordered to be in complete darkness on selected nights when the blackout drill was signaled by a loud, squawking siren that resounded throughout the city. All lights were to be turned out everywhere for an hour or two, and families waited in total darkness, perhaps huddled around a radio, awaiting the all-clear siren again. The drill was monitored and enforced by volunteers called air raid wardens, who patrolled the neighborhoods making sure that darkness reigned. At times, we could hear a voice call out, "turn out your light!"

However, we children in the Scalzi household were not preoccupied with a bomb or two landing on our heads; we feared, instead, the dreaded Blackout that lurked in the darkness of our home! Our world of the comics was peopled with Dick Tracy, Orphan Annie, Mutt & Jeff and superheroes such as Batman, Superman, Captain Marvel, Captain America…but, *The Blackout?*

When the air raid siren sounded, our world was in blackness. My parents sat by the radio and Mario, Vincent and I ran for cover - under a bed, in a closet or by Mom and Pop. The Blackout would soon make its appearance. When it passed a window, we saw the scary silhouette of a hooded figure carrying its "bopper," rumored to be a sock with a golf ball inside. The creature wandered the darkened rooms looking for prey, and when it cornered a victim, the result was a bop on the head. Of course, we ran to our parents to complain about brother Lou, but when the lights came on again, he always proclaimed his innocence.

Eventually, the lights, indeed, went on again "all over the world". The war was over and. life resumed once more. My high school years were musically marked with the tunes of Frankie Lane, Tony Bennett, Nat King Cole, Teresa Brewer, Joni James, Johnny Ray and other classic favorites. I associated their melodies with memorable people and events from those precious years of my youth. "Anytime" by Eddie Fisher had its special meaning for me as did some Kay Starr musical hits, such as "Wheel of fortune."

Those high school years were not noteworthy for any memorable scholarship on my part. I was a bit lazy, easily distracted and very much the daydreamer, but my imagination was quite fertile. I do remember that lazy, hot June afternoon, slumped at my school desk, unproductive as ever and waiting for the 3:30 dismissal bell. The study hall doors were wide open to allow some airflow from the hallway. We could hear the Poughkeepsie High School band, under the direction of Mr. Hawkins, practicing in the auditorium. A haunting melody floated into the room and caught my attention. It was so exotic and seductive; it seemed to beckon me and to draw me away to unknown and mysterious lands of camels and robed people. "In a Persian market," composed by Albert Ketelbey, was to be for me a clarion call that would launch me on a lifelong love affair with world travel. I was soon to answer that call.

Every year as graduation day approached in June, our high school presented a program called Moving up Day. The freshmen, sophomore, junior and senior classes each put on skits, sang songs and generally shared good times. We concluded the day with each group singing a rather wistful, sentimental tune about moving on in the stages of life. The freshman class sang, "Where, oh where are the friendly freshmen? - Safe now in the sophomore world." We concluded with "Where, oh where are the grand old seniors? - Safe now in the wide, wide world." I've sometimes wondered about that last line.

Jo Stafford warbled "You belong to me," a popular tune riding high on the music charts and solidly recorded in my memory. You see, it came along when I experienced my first romantic relationship and that was with Sally, a pretty, brown-eyed young lady from nearby Wappinger Falls. The song brings back to me our stroll one evening along Middlebush Road and that first kiss, seated on a stone wall. The melody followed me into the

Navy where it took on more meaning because the words spoke of travelling to far-off lands but with the reminder that "you belong to me".

Graduation launched us into young adulthood and for many of us, that meant military service.

In basic training at Bainbridge Naval Training Center in Maryland, we marched and drilled to "Bridge on the River Kwai" and "Stars and Stripes forever". Certainly, our unofficial "anthem" was the spirited, ever-youthful "Anchors aweigh." Popular tunes of that stage of military service were nostalgic songs such as "Wish you were here" and "P.S. I love you." Another was Eartha Kitt's enticing "C'est si bon."

Along the way, I have gathered in my memory and heart what I call "mood melodies". They vividly paint an image of a memorable person or moment or a meaningful place in my travels. A good example is the previously mentioned "In a Persian market" and the wistful, nostalgic "Intermezzo" from the Mascagni opera Cavalleria Rusticana. Augustin Lara's "Granada" never fails to stir me and has always been a favorite of mine. A feeling of excitement and anticipation swelled within me as the train rolled into the station of that historic and fabled city. Within me played the melody and the words *guitarras romanticas* and *lindas mujeres*, but the bubble burst when I left the train at my destination and was met with, not romantic guitars and lovely women, but several workers busily unloading a supply of toilet bowls and bidets from a truck.

I found myself enjoying a warm, sunny day relaxing in London's St. James Park. The band entertained the gathering with popular melodies, lively marches and several classical favorites. The program concluded with the band playing an impressive rendition of "God save the Queen," which is, of course, the national anthem of The United Kingdom and an admirable one, indeed.

Traveling about, I became familiar with the anthems of several nations and have compared and rated them. My favorites are those of Germany, Russia, Israel, France and the U.K. France's "La Marseillaise" and Italy's "Fratelli d'Italia" are rousing, uplifting rallying calls, while Germany's "Deutschland Uber Alles" and the UK's are majestic and soaring. I find the Israeli anthem to be striking and moving in its religious qualities and mood. It is like a chant, a solemn hymn from the pages of the Old Testament.

Yes, I have also entertained the idea of putting together a homemade recording of this musical diary. It would be a personal endeavor, meaningful to and appreciated by me and me alone; it would never see the light of day in the marketplace. The recording would incorporate portions of preferably original recordings. Strung along chronologically, the tunes become a flowing, uninterrupted story of a lifetime, told in music.

The performances would be infrequent and come to me when the mood or occasion presents itself. I envision a cold, snowy evening, settled comfortably in a soft chair by a cozy fire, sipping a cup of hot chocolate. I reach into the library of my mind or draw forth my recording and depart on a nostalgic, melodic getaway. No passport or packing of luggage necessary, and it is free of airport hassle. I will see beautiful people once again, relive phases of growing up and the wondrous experiences of globetrotting days. It is simply *Bon voyage* and off I go on a happy, exciting musical journey of, literally, a lifetime.

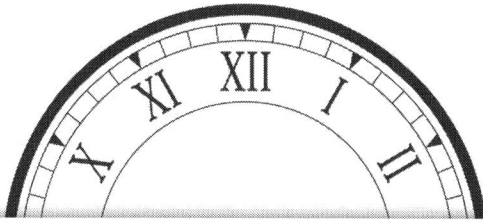

# Close Calls

One is not strong who never falls,
But who falls and rises again.
-Anonymous

*Stars over Sydney*

Maccarelli's lumberyard sat across the street from our Home Street apartment building, but it was more than a lumberyard for us street urchins; it was the neighborhood playground, well - furnished with a dilapidated shack, piles of lumber (some with protruding nails) and other assorted debris strewn about the grounds. We spent long hours climbing over the lumber and up onto the roof or hanging out in the shanty clubhouse. Everything else was left to our imaginations.

The urchins consisted of a gaggle of local lads, among them representatives of the O'Shay clan, a DeMarte or two and those Scalzi kids. We were divided, unofficially, into the "big kids"...Baby John" O'Shay and my brother Lou, to name a couple…and "the squirts" who tried to belong but were barely tolerated. Our ranks included Buster Jefferson, Henry O'Shay, my brothers Mario and Vincent and myself. Buster was my little Black buddy who lived next door and would come to share with me, at the tender age of six, my first harrowing adventure.

At the far end of Maccarelli's stood a small building immediately behind Sheffield's Milk Company. There was a low-lying, sloping roof on one end which was accessible for climbing and romping. Buster and I were reluctantly hoisted up so that we might join the fun with the big boys. One day, there emerged from a rooftop trap door a rather large-sized company man who roared and proceeded to scatter the group in all directions. Everyone scurried to the edge of the roof and easily jumped to safety; everyone but little Buster and little Bart. We stood there shaking, frightened and frozen at the roof's edge. The others shouted, "Jump! Jump!", but it might as well have been Mount Everest; we could not find the courage to make the perilous leap. We stood there terrified and quivering until we fell into the clutches of the burly brute who lectured the boys below and then lowered us to the ground. Buster and I had survived a most frightening episode and, in a true spirit of equality and brotherhood, had shed copious tears together - and wet our pants! We could not return to our homes in such a deplorable condition, so the big kids made a fire to dry our clothes and then send us on our way. With the passing of time, the trauma of the lumberyard episode gradually faded away and I moved on with life and all the joys and sorrows, lumps and bumps that awaited me.

It had been an enjoyable and exciting day on a safari some miles out of Nairobi, and I had seen a good share of lions, hippos, giraffes, elephants - even a cluster of vultures - out there in the Kenyan savannah. It was time to return to my hotel room, shower and relax for the evening, feeling quite satisfied with my day well-spent. I picked up several postcards and stamps and retired to my comfortable, air-conditioned room. I filled those cards with accounts of my African adventures and then decided to mail them that evening; there was a mailbox around the corner. As I came out of the elevator and into the lobby, popping sounds could be heard coming from the street.

Turning the corner, I saw an excited crowd gathered around, of all things, a large pool of blood on the sidewalk. I inquired and was told that a foreigner, from Uganda, had tried to rob a shop and when pursued by the police, resisted and was shot dead on the spot. There were bullet holes in the walls and several cars, indicating that there had been a grand shootout. If I had arrived but minutes earlier, I might have been caught in the gunfire and ended my travel days forever. It saddened me to see the blood and to think that a human life had been extinguished on that sidewalk. When I applied some of my enlightened American compassion and commented to others that the police could have shot him in the legs instead, I received a quick response. Several Kenyans were annoyed and explained that, after all, the guy was a robber, had resisted, and the policemen were justified in killing him. They wanted nothing of my know- it-all American wisdom and sense of justice. I returned to my room with a lesson learned: When in Kenya do as the Kenyans do! Indeed.

A regional train returned me to Barcelona following a pleasant day spent in Mirasol with Anna, Jordi and their families. They often escaped the summer heat and city buzz by relaxing at their cozy home in the tranquil suburban community overlooking the big town. The train deposited me near the city center and I made my way up the Ramblas promenade on a lovely, comfortable evening.

I quickly realized that the usually bustling, pulsating Ramblas was transformed. The streets, walkways and shops were eerily deserted and an uncomfortable silence was in the air. It was only ten o'clock, an hour when normally the delightful, picturesque, tree-lined Ramblas promenade is a showcase of strollers, tables of diners and entertaining street performers. *Que pasa aqui?* As I proceeded up the center walkway I saw, just ahead of me, a phalanx of helmeted riot police, armed to the teeth. In one side street, a police barricade was holding back an angry, cursing, gesticulating mob of protesters. The streets and curbs were strewn with those nasty, hard-rubber bullets.

Wrong place at the wrong time! The scenario resembled something out of "High Noon" with the riot police on one end and I on the other. I must have provoked them and seemed like an arrogant, defiant demonstrator because, out of nowhere, a burly policeman was upon me, shouting, "Corre! Corre!" (Run! Run!) and accompanying his commands with a hefty swing of his rubber club across my buttocks! Of course, I could no longer run and I was forced to limp back to my nearby hotel. I thought of how seriously I could have been injured if the club had been aimed at my head or if I had been the target of one of those rubber bullets. When I requested my room key at the desk, I also asked what the Spanish word was for that damned club that almost crippled me. I, a Spanish language teacher back home, thought it was *baston*, but the concierge at the desk corrected me. That night I retired to my room with an aching backside and a new Spanish vocabulary word. I learned it the hard way, but I shall not easily forget the word *porra*..

July 7 marks the start of the seven-day San Fermin festival in Pamplona, Spain and it is one merry, lively and free-wheeling party of singing, drinking, eating and dancing in the streets. The saint remains faintly remembered or honored, while the daily running of the bulls is the stuff of daring recklessness and frivolous heroics. Each morning, a lively group of "crazies" gathers at one end of a long, winding, barricaded street, awaiting the signal that would launch the running. Precisely at seven, a shot rings out and the runners burst forward; a second signal releases the bulls from a corral and they come rumbling down, quickly gaining ground on the runners. "I can do this," I said to myself and joined the crazies. Along the route, several runners were bowled over while others escaped peril by leaping onto the street barriers or into doorways. I managed to avoid an approaching horned tank by clinging to a lamppost.

Both runners and bulls entered the arena to the cheers of the assembled crowd. The animals moved to a pen where they remained enclosed until turned loose, one at a time, into the gathering of taunting runners. The first angry toro made furious charges and scattered the would-be matadors in all directions. Suddenly, it changed course, aimed its horns towards several of us and charged. I ran for my life, stumbled and fell in its path. I covered my head and curled up into a fetal position while big bad bull proceeded to toss me in the sand like a rag doll. Fortunately for me, the animal turned away to pursue another tormenting runner. I limped back to my hotel with torn jeans, a bloody knee and grateful that the sun was shining and I was still on this planet.

I do not always go courting danger or misfortune; there are times when it comes seeking me out. In the lovely city of Sydney in September of 2012, I came face-to-face with my mortality, like never before in my life. Linda and I were completing a marvelous month experiencing the wonders of Australia. We had visited Adelaide, Alice Springs, Melbourne and Canberra. Yes, all those unique creatures really did exist - kangaroos, of course, but also the platybus, wombat, koala, echidna, wallaby, emu and the kookaburra bird. We saw them and we marveled at them.

We planned to enjoy Sydney and then conclude with Brisbane and our return flight to USA; we never made it to Brisbane. Down to Sydney harbor we went, to an area called The Rocks where we visited a collection of bungalows from the early colonial era of Australian history. Linda wanted to tour inside while I could not turn away from that glorious sun. "Enjoy the tour, Mou," I said. "I'll relax out here and watch the world go by." I chose to sit atop a low brick wall nearby and proceeded to jump back and up onto the ledge, propelling myself over the wall and down six feet on the other side. I landed head-first onto a concrete pavement. My vision was dim and fuzzy, my hearing was an in-and-out buzzing sound. Several kind and caring Australians came to assist me and, fortunately, I managed to mumble "Linda", pointing towards the bungalows.

The ambulance rushed us off to St. Vincent's Hospital where the diagnosis was skull fracture, linear spine fracture and hematoma by the brain, requiring surgery. Released after two weeks, we returned to The Rocks and stood where I recall saying, "This is where I nearly ended my life." My recovery was total and I attribute my survival and return to good health to three factors: to my loving guardian angel Linda, to the excellent care and services at St. Vincent's Hospital and to my Calabrian heritage. In Italy, people of the Calabria region in the south are considered hard-headed and obstinate; I passed that test.

Robert Burns wrote of "The best laid plans of mice and men" gone awry and such was the case one summer during a visit to Caracas, Venezuela. I joined a couple of German adventurers who had made plans to explore the interior of Venezuela and visit villages, the rain forest, and perhaps go fishing for piranhas. After an exciting day of exploration and discovery, we prepared for the return journey to Caracas. Night had descended upon us and we had many miles to travel. The narrow mountain road took us through the vast rain forest on a silent, solitary drive interrupted occasionally by a chorus of chirping tree frogs performing high up on the forest "roof".

We watched a vehicle approach and pass us, then round the mountain ahead of us and disappear into the night. When we arrived at that point, we rounded the mountain curve and discovered that the road had ended abruptly! There was rain forest where a road should have been. One of my companions announced that there had been a mudslide. What had become of the other car? Did it make it through? Was it buried and lost? I must have sounded naive when I suggested that we grab our shovels and start digging away to open the road. They explained that the mountainside had come down and that there were tons of mud and trees in front of us. Not good. Their real fear was that we had to leave immediately, going back the way we came and taking the long road around to Caracas. Another mudslide could have blocked our retreat and trapped us or, worse, buried us alive! it was a long ride back before sighting the welcoming lights of Caracas and civilization.

A few years ago, I came full circle when I made a nostalgic pilgrimage to White Plains and the old haunts of my childhood. The brick apartment building and several houses had vanished from a now-truncated Home Street, but Maccarelli's lumberyard was still there, albeit in a shabby, desolate state of existence. I made my way to the far end of the yard and paused at the scene of my long-ago nightmare. I smiled as I gazed upon a ledge that was no higher than five feet off the ground! I could almost hear Buster Jefferson chuckling from somewhere in this world - or the other.

# Irks, Quirks... and Jerks

What fools these mortals be.
-William Shakespeare (1564-1616)
*A midsummer night's dream*

It is not all peaches and cream, this big, wide world we live in. William Shakespeare aptly called it a stage and he populated it with an assortment of fancy and foolish mortals playing an infinity of diverse roles.

I have long despised line jumpers and cursed bureaucracy and red tape. I loathe airport delays and interminable security measures, and as I get older, the list has lengthened substantially. I don't cope well with floppy plastic bags nor with packages and products that are near-impossible to open. Receiving those cursed robot phone calls is infuriating and I condemn airlines which increasingly charge fees for everything short of the use of their toilets...so far.

Some cultural differences can be puzzling and annoying, as well. On a first trip to Europe, I entered a public restroom in a Paris train station and beheld a woman with bucket and mop nonchalantly cleaning the urinals while several men, also nonchalantly, went about their personal business. I hastily retreated and fled in search of relief elsewhere.

And there is no shortage of the disturbing "types" that cross our paths and can make life miserable. I boarded my first ship, USS Seneca, in 1953 at Norfolk, Virginia. The ship was going to sea, to Guantanamo Bay, Cuba, and that was to be my first time on the high seas. One shipmate, a loud-mouthed, obnoxious fellow from Ohio, took a disliking for me and dedicated much time tormenting me with insults and sneers. I was a shy youngster from upstate New York with no sea duty experience and this gave him license to play the role of "Old Salt" and dominate me. During the cruise, he approached me and announced with a snarl that he was waiting for a storm at sea so that he could watch me getting seasick and vomiting before his eyes. He lived for that moment.

A day out of port and a punishing storm fell upon us with a merciless fury. It was my misfortune that my duty for that night was to do a four-hour watch on the bridge together with my nemesis: he at the helm and I at the radar scope nearby. Looking back, I do believe that he had convinced someone to make that arrangement. The ship tossed and heaved and my tormentor at the wheel anxiously kept his eye on me, waiting to see me fall apart. In the darkness of the pilot house he could not see the greenish tint that covered my suffering face, nor could he imagine the agony I was enduring. He would have been very pleased. Obstinately, I refused to give him the satisfaction of seeing me vomit before him, so I was determined to persevere and, ultimately, I succeeded in surviving the four-hour agony. I left the bridge and made it to a sink where I gushed out my guts and what looked like my liver. It was, for me, victory at sea, but at a heavy price. The satisfaction, however, was immeasurable. As a side note, I later had the pleasure of meeting the guy in a port bar and taking a swing at his ugly face.

On a crowded train bound for the city of Catanzaro in southern Italy, I was lucky to find a seat, and I settled down in my compartment for the long journey ahead. At a stop along the route, a young woman carrying a little baby opened the compartment door and, in an imploring tone, inquired about a seat. "Si. signora. Certamente," responded two gentlemen who quickly vacated their seats and took their places in the hot, crowded corridor. She was most grateful and everyone was happy. However, we soon became witnesses to a gradual transformation of our compartment as she proceeded to "dress" the area with hanging diapers and bottles and powders everywhere. Mother then asked to shut the compartment window because the breeze might bother the baby. So, we sat in a stifling hot steam room as the baby slept peacefully. The defining moment came when the train made another stop and picked up more passengers. A weary traveler came to our compartment and asked, "Is there a seat for me?" It was Dragon Lady, already occupying three spaces, who quickly called out, "No. No room here." I watched as the poor guy retreated into the packed corridor. When the train entered the Catanzaro station, I left the nursery room, having witnessed how The Madonna with child had morphed into Attila the Hun.

There is a specimen I call "The Worm" and who may be found lurking wherever people gather to form a line. He's the guy who, while you've waited patiently and long to purchase that train ticket, shuffles about casually, glancing here and there, then maneuvers ever more closely, and when all are lulled into distraction, oozes into the line. When caught, I enjoy watching him unceremoniously shamed to the back of the line. There was one worm who was caught jumping the line and protested that he had to buy a train ticket, as if we were waiting there to order pizza. A chorus of scorn accompanied his humiliating retreat.

Not in my wildest dreams could I imagine that I, the wise and seasoned traveler, would ever be sucked into a scam. My nephew Ed was doing a year of cultural exchange teaching English at Shenzhen University in China, and I joined him for a week, during which time we taught some classes together. Well, I got scammed and in a manner that was very clever, but which left me spitting mad! At a street corner, two young men approached us offering to exchange money at a very favorable rate. Such dealings are strictly forbidden in China and we were at great risk when we agreed to the transaction. I handed him fifty dollars after I had the proper amount of Chinese yuan in my hand. While we chatted amiably, I observed the money holder playing with the bill, folding and unfolding it in intricate patterns. I watched him carefully because I was no fool. Not I. Suddenly, the other fellow shouted, "Police!" and we prepared to scatter. False alarm, I guess. No police. At this point the two decided not to exchange and we each returned the money we held. "Zai jen". See ya.

Ed and I moved on down the street and I unfolded the cleverly folded fifty-dollar bill. I gazed upon a miserable, solitary dollar bill! The bandit had this one already folded in his pocket and ready to be switched when we turned for the police. Oh, I was angry, and we went searching the neighborhood; I badly wanted to make chop suey of them or just kick them in the won tons! Oh, well...my pride wounded, wallet deflated and lesson learned.

Does a traveler exist who hasn't had a tale to tell of a problem regarding baggage, check-in and airport security? I no longer check in my bag for any flight to anywhere. It's one carry-on bag, thank you, and it flies with me near where I sit. Checking in at Leonardo DaVinci (Fiumicino) Airport for a flight to Bucharest, Romania should have been a routine, nothing procedure. It was nearing lunch time and the check-in agent fussed with tags, boarding passes and luggage, while he babbled with another agent nearby about eating a plump mozzarella and enjoying a glass of wine for lunch. "This guy is going to screw up here," I thought, "His mind is on munching a mozzarella and not on my bag". We landed at Otopeni Airport in Bucharest and my bag was nowhere to be found. For three days I managed and survived with some basic dental and shaving essentials I bought locally. When my bag eventually appeared, it had travelled via Helsinki, Finland. What could I say except to hope that his mozzarella lunch had been for him a little episode of indigestion.

His name was Smitty and we did not like each other, plain and simple. We never saw eye to eye performing our duties on USS Salinan in Key West, Florida. I had been transferred from another ship and came aboard to assume duties as head yeoman in the ship's office. That did not sit well with my assistant Smitty. Although lower in rank, he had been aboard two years and resented the intrusion of this newcomer. A simple assignment given him was met with, "We never do it this way" or "I've been in this office two years and..." I endured his arrogance and pouting for several months until I received welcome orders for transfer to USS Marias in Barcelona, Spain.

My orders were for me to spend a week home and then proceed to the Mediterranean to board my new ship. I packed my sea bag and, before departing USS Salinan, I made the rounds bidding farewell to all my shipmates (except Smitty, of course). Although I was young and strong, the journey home lugging my heavy sea bag through airports and train stations, was a struggle. At home I emptied my bag so that Mom could wash my clothes for the trip to sunny Spain. What a surprise when I found that someone had stuffed in my bag a huge iron link from an anchor chain; it must have weighed eighty pounds! Smitty, that sleazy sea slug, had gotten the last word.

Things have gotten reasonably better when traveling in Italy, but there was a time - oh, there was a time when this blessed land of my heritage was, unquestionably, the royal realm of red tape and the bedrock of bureaucracy. Changing money, purchasing a ticket, or making inquiries almost certainly guaranteed generous portions of confusion, run-around and the shuffling of papers. I experienced a money exchange transaction where I was called to window A, sent to window C, then to another for a stamp and signature and finally to the cashier for the money. I compared it to a similar transaction in Germany where, mercifully, it was simply one-two-three.

Perhaps, after all is said and done, irks, quirks and jerks are here to stay and are, unfortunately, an essential part of the human experience. Yes, life may be a stage, but more like a merry-go-round version from which we cannot alight, so we bear it and share it and go around for the ride.

*Culture shock*

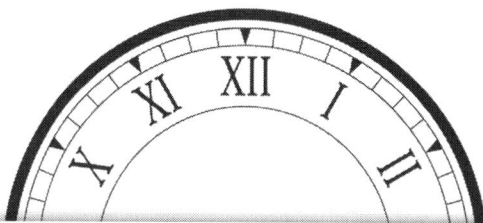

# Here lies...

The boast of heraldry, the pomp of power
And all that wealth e'er gave
Awaits alike the inevitable hour....
The paths of glory lead but to the grave.
-Thomas Gray (1716-1771)
*Elegy written in a country churchyard*

Stranger...
Pause as you pass by -
As you are now,
so once was I.
As I am now,
so must you be.
Do bid farewell
and follow me...

Nothing morbid about my nature; merely possessing a superabundance of curiosity that over the years has drawn me to a cemetery or two.

We youngsters occasionally meandered down to the Poughkeepsie Rural Cemetery where we spent long, lazy summer afternoons wandering and exploring among the gravestones, searching for the oldest resident there, reading epitaphs or amusing ourselves by rhyming names. One day we came across the titillating combination of Mowell, Howell, and Powell; another day it was Mink, Dink and Fink. One of our group was called Fab (his three initials) and he was amused by our reaction when he led us to a stone and showed his family plot. His mom and dad had their names and their birthdates clearly displayed, but so was our young buddy's. We groaned, he chuckled. Fab has since filled that patch of God's green earth.

The Rural Cemetery is a beautiful expanse of lovely trees, rolling hills, winding paths and a serene pond inhabited by a community of graceful swans and waddling ducks. A narrow road climbs a hill to a summit which provides a stunning view of the scenic Hudson River below. To many, this point has been known as Lover's Leap, so named because a local legend has it that long ago, two young Indian lovers, meeting with disapproval from their parents, tragically leaped to their deaths. It was, indeed, a touching tale for me - until my later Navy days when a shipmate of another state related a similar story from his region. So much for that legend.

We were young, carefree and happy living in the moment with not a hint of a profound thought about life or mortality nor about the famous and the infamous who had been players on the world stage. Curiosity, however, was germinating in my soul; an awareness was blossoming and questions were beginning to take shape. Who were these good souls lying at our feet? Did they not once laugh and play and weep as we? Had they not joked or played a prank or spent happy times at a barbecue or danced at a wedding? Was this a young soldier who had left his sweetheart to go off to a distant land and fight one of those wars? Do these markers remember a talented musician, an inventor, perhaps a beloved teacher? Did this fellow have a lofty goal and did he achieve it before he was summoned away from this earthly existence? Stopping at a small stone alongside the road to Lover's Leap, I read the inscription *Elizabeth Lee Bentley, April 15, 1944*. I was moved by the tender words that followed: *To know her was to love her.* Again, the questions. What had she done to have been so loved? Was she a favorite aunt or loving sister? I recall thinking that I wished I could have met her.

*Ils furent que nous sommes. Nous serons ce qu'ils sont* are the words above the entrance to Pere Lachaise Cemetery in an eastern district of Paris. *They were what once were we. As they are now so shall we be,* somberly inviting the visitor to walk among the resting places of some of the greatest figures in human history. It is a silent city of the dead but the residents who repose there once rocked the world and stirred the hearts and souls of countless millions. They left their indelible mark and we are in awe. Over the years of wandering among these sleeping greats, I have paused to contemplate their accomplishments, their fame or infamy, and to record in my memory my very first emotional impression and reaction.

## Napoleon Bonaparte (1769-1821)

The dust has long settled, the smoke cleared and the turmoil subsided where once armies marched and cannons roared across the European continent in the early 19th century. He shook the very foundations of the world in a century immersed in revolutions, inventions, the emergence of new nations, political and economic upheaval, and giants in the realms of music, theater and literature. Napoleon not only left his mark in history, but his influence has resonated to the present day. He was a military genius, a relentless reformer and a controversial but well-meaning ruler. His military exploits and strategies are studied in military schools, and elements of his Code are prominent and relevant to the present day.

Napoleon escaped from his exile on the island of Elba and reorganized his armies for a dramatic return to warfare and conquest. Defeat at Waterloo resulted in his being shipped off to the remote island of St Helena in the South Atlantic. He died there in exile in 1821 and his cremated remains were brought back to France to be among his people, as he had requested. After a career of campaigns, exiles, escapes, expeditions, Bonaparte has been contained, put to rest in a red granite esophagus in the rotunda at Les Invalides in Paris. This, I thought, was surely "for keeps."

## Abraham Lincoln (1809-1865)

On Tuesday, April 25, 1865, President Abraham Lincoln paid a visit to Poughkeepsie, New York, but I missed him by about 150 years. The funeral train was making its way from Washington, DC on its way to the final resting place in Springfield, Illinois. In May of 2014, I returned the courtesy and traveled to Springfield to pay homage to this beloved man. He has been my favorite president and I had long dreamed of making this pilgrimage.

Standing at the tomb, my fertile mind drifted off to a scenario in which I sat with the president and asked him several questions: "What were your deepest feelings when the cannons erupted at Fort Sumter beginning the Civil War or when you signed the Emancipation Proclamation?" "What were your concerns and doubts about the great national divide and the unfolding events of that bloody war?" I would have certainly been entertained by his earthy, down-home wit and his humble, yet profound philosophy and wisdom. If I could have summoned or assembled a band or choir I would have honored the occasion with a stirring rendition of *Battle Hymn of the Republic*, a favorite of the president.

☉☉☉☉☉☉

Others commanded no armies, conquered no lands, moved no mountains, yet uniquely touched and soothed a weary world.

## Frederic Chopin (1810-1840)

My first visit was accidental. I was casually browsing among the gravesites at Pere Lachaise making discoveries. A short distance from where I had paused to read an inscription, there was a small group gathered around a monument. Curiosity moved me to approach and see; I found myself in the presence of the great Chopin. After over 150 years, the faithful continue to come, bearing fresh flowers, as if he were but recently interred. His life was abbreviated, but in the short time allotted to him. he blessed the world with music so sublime and immortal!

However, fully paying homage to the man requires a further step - a visit to Holy Cross Church in Warsaw, where his heart is enshrined and memorialized with the inscription:

## Frederic Chopin

Son of Poland and music,
His heart rests in its bosom..

## Giuseppe Garibaldi (1807-1882)

The ferry approached the tiny island of Caprera, a clump of land sitting off the coast of mainland Sardinia. Once disembarked, I made my way up a hill and stopped before a humble country structure nestled in a rustic courtyard of gnarled trees and scattered flowers. Nearby I spotted a plain, rather nondescript stone that marked the final resting place of Giuseppe Garibaldi. Except for the rustling of the trees in a gentle breeze, a reverent silence and serenity reigned. But, here in eternal repose, was a man by no means simple, silent and reserved. His heroism, courage and ferocity in the cause of independence and the unity of Italy, crowned him with the merited title of "The Lion of Caprera".

He fought legendary battles from one end of the boot peninsula to the other, always outnumbered by the enemy but never subdued. The insurgents repelled the meddling of Austria, France and the Papal States, and modern Italy was born in 1870. Ever restless and adventurous, Garibaldi joined forces in South America fighting for the independence of Uruguay; and gaining the title "Hero of Two Worlds". My thoughts as I paused at his gravesite? The lion sleeps..

## Vladimir Lenin (1870-1924)

A long, orderly line of the faithful and the curious shuffles across Red Square and feeds slowly into the red granite mausoleum that is the sepulcher of Vladimir Lenin, once the centerpiece of the Bolshevik Revolution of 1917 and the father of Soviet Communism. Under this man and the monster Stalin, the "Socialist paradise" brought suffering and death to millions of people. Vladimir went before the Almighty for judgement in 1924; his body was embalmed and placed on public display.

Entering the funeral chamber, one is engulfed in an eerie red glow which also bathes Lenin's goatee-bearded, stern face. What was striking to me was that firm, clenched right fist resting on his chest. He seemed to be warning, "Beware! I am watching you!"

☺☺☺☺☺☺

71

The quest for the resting places of the great figures of history does not always bear fruit. Call them empty tombs.

The gospel of Luke informs us that the crucified Jesus was taken down and placed for burial in the personal tomb of a follower, Joseph of Arimathea. Of course, according to Holy Scripture, the tomb was vacated in three days and today the Church of the Holy Sepulcher exists over the spot where tradition claims that Jesus was entombed.

In a different manner, there is not a tomb nor gravesite that enshrines the remains of Joan of Arc, warrior-saint of the 15th century. Amazingly, a 19-year-old girl, in armor, led the armies of France to victory over the English and crowned the king of France! I traveled to Rouen in northwest France to stand before the mound where in 1431 Joan of Arc was burned at the stake and her remains cast into the river.

Enter the Cathedral of Seville in Spain and you will see four large stone figures representing the four Spanish kingdoms of Castille, Aragon, Navarra and Leon. On their shoulders they bear a casket with the remains of the great explorer Christopher Columbus. Really? A cathedral in Santo Domingo, The Dominican Republic, claims to hold the mortal remains of - Christopher Columbus! Hmmmmmmmm.....

Pursuing the Gospel narration of the miracle at Bethany, I came to the small village, not far from Jerusalem's walls, knowing full-well that the main players would be absent. I simply wanted to be there to contemplate and reflect upon the long-ago biblical event. I descended a narrow stone stairway and paused in a small antechamber which faced the burial chamber. There, about 2000 years ago, Jesus called out, "Lazarus, come forth!" Very moving!

Whereas a most grateful world would happily welcome a magnificent tomb in his honor, no one has succeeded in unlocking the mystery and answering the question, "Where is Wolfgang Amadeus Mozart?"

☺☺☺☺☺☺

On the lighter side:

Wandering along the paths and walkways of a necropolis, a city of the dead, one understandably expects an ambience of gray and gloom, a somber numbness of reverence and respect; but there are moments that can be rather amusing, to say the least.

Stop at the Pere Lachaise cemetery gravesite of Victor Noir, who was shot and killed in a duel in 1870. Sprawled atop the tomb is the bronze image of the French journalist, lying on his back, legs spread and hat nearby. What is prominent is a rather polished lump located in the area of Victor's genitalia. There exists a fertility cult where some women of Paris come to the tomb to rub the lump with the hope of marriage or the birth of a baby. Hands-on therapy, I guess.

Oscar Wilde, the flamboyant 19th century Irish poet and playwright, was truly "one for the books." He was witty, bold and self-destructive. His brash, openly gay lifestyle was the cause of much controversy and it clashed with the mores and sensitivities of the time, especially with the authorities. Appropriately, the figure depicted on the marble tomb shows a sublime free spirit, representative of the poet. What is amusing, if not puzzling, is that the monument is covered with the lip prints of women who have visited and showered Oscar with kisses.

A resident of Novodevichy Cemetery in Moscow is the cold war leader of the former Soviet Union, Nikita Khrushchev. Some of his quotations were notable for their defiance, bombast and braggadocio in defense of Communism and condemnation of Capitalism. He mocked, "We will weaken your economy until you fall like over-ripe fruit into our hands" and "We will keep feeding you small doses of Socialism until you wake up to find that you already have Communism," And his most famous quote, made in 1956? "Whether you like it or not, *we will bury you.*" I moved on with a parting thought, "Sorry, Nikita, we buried *you.*"

☺☺☺☺☺☺

## Mumtaz Mahal (1593-1631)

Its architectural grandeur and beauty are stunning, it is a breathtaking marvel in ivory white marble, it is a monument to love and...it is a tomb. The Mogul emperor of India, Shah Jehan, built the Taj Mahal in Agra between 1632 and 1645 for his favorite wife, Mumtaz Mahal, whom he loved dearly and for whom he grieved so deeply. The perfect love story was sealed when eventually the emperor was entombed by her side.

In a more mundane frame of mind, I could not avoid other thoughts as

I wandered through the monument and its gardens. This incredibly lavish and costly memorial was constructed to honor one solitary human being while the surrounding masses, as today, coped with their humble lives of poverty and deprivation. No one can ever say that life is fair.

## Adelina Patti (1843-1919)

She was born in Madrid, Spain to traveling Italian opera performers, spent her early childhood in lower New York City, captivated crowds in cities across continents, settled in Wales and now lies in Pere Lachaise in Paris. She was the celebrated 19th century soprano who dazzled the opera world with her lovely voice, flamboyant lifestyle, and the exorbitant fees she demanded - and received. She sang for Queen Victoria, charmed the royal pants off Russia's Tsar Alexander II, crossed the United States on a singing tour, riding in her own private, luxurious railway car. She once sat backstage with one shoe on, refusing to perform until the frazzled impresario could come up with the guaranteed high fee. When the audience finally filled the seats to capacity, she put on the other shoe and went on to perform.

But "Her Majesty" once received a rare rebuke and it came from the great composer, Gioacchino Rossini. At one of his lavish parties attended by celebrities of the world of the arts, Adelina was asked to perform a famous Rossini piece, which she proceeded to execute with much embellishment and an over-abundance of coloratura. When she concluded, the Master calmly said to her, "Beautiful, Adelina. By the way, what is it called?" Yes, that was Adelina Patti, renown Queen of Song. In her glory days I would not have been worthy enough to approach her or be in her royal presence. Yet, there I was humbly brushing away the dust and dried leaves from her marble tomb.

ⓒⓒⓒⓒⓒ

*On the curious side.*

Fate often chooses to be fickle and play its games even after one sheds his mortal trappings and, at least theoretically, goes to rest in peace. The mausoleum in Pere Lachaise reads "Rossini" where the great composer was

74

interred in 1868. His French wife, Olympe later joined him for eternity, but not quite so, because today Olympe sleeps alone. Several years after their passing, Italy launched a campaign to have Rossini returned to his native soil. He was removed and now rests in the Santa Croce church in Florence. Olympe, however, chose to remain undisturbed in her native soil, as well.

An even more poignant account, rather poetic in itself, involves the British poets Robert and Elizabeth Browning. Their exchange of poems of love and devotion are well-known to and appreciated by all followers of English literature. Elizabeth Barrett was a sickly young lady whose homebound existence limited her to writing poetry. We know that Robert Browning visited the Barretts, fell in love with Elizabeth and took her away from her unhappy world. They lived in Italy, wrote verses and enjoyed life immensely. Theirs was a truly beautiful love story, but for the ending.

Today, Robert Browning reposes in Poets Corner in London's Westminster Abbey while Elizabeth Barrett Browning can be found in the Protestant Cemetery in Florence, Italy. They were supposed to be together, but the Barrett family thought otherwise.

## Mao Tse Tung (1893-1976)

The procession that has moved across the stage of Chinese history and culture has been a veritable showcase of astounding personalities and monumental achievements. Chairman Mao can lay claim to several deeds, as well. "The Great Helmsman" did indeed lead a massive revolution in a brutal, bloody struggle that united the masses and formed the Communist People's Republic of China. He thereby came to rule the largest "empire" in Chinese history.

Visitors can pay their respects or satisfy their curiosity by taking their place in line in Tiananmen Square and entering a large hall where the body is on display. The guards allow no pauses and urge the people to move along quickly. I needed to return to the entrance and get back in line for another look. His ample body, draped in the national flag, is in a glass-topped casket in the center of the hall.

☺☺☺☺☺☺

And so the globe turns. The ebb and flow of world events, the glories and follies of mankind continue on their appointed course while on a quiet slope in a Poughkeepsie cemetery, Elizabeth Lee Bentley reposes in eternal peace.

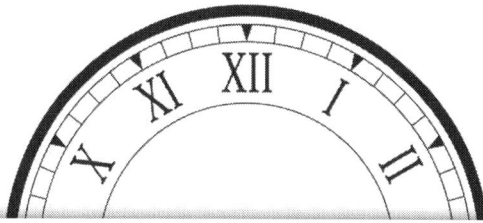

# Has anyone seen God?

God wants spiritual fruit,
Not religious nuts.
-Anonymous

Mother Teresa – A saint for all seasons.

A little boy had passed away, and for some time a respectful silence lingered among the smattering of families in our small Home Street neighborhood. I was a mere seven years of age when young Tonio left us and I could not fully grasp the meaning of death, although it did sink in that the boy was gone and was not coming back ever again. Questions churned in my puzzled mind. Why did he die? Where had he gone? Why did his mom and dad let him go away? For me, death simply meant the loss of a pet cat or finding a dead bird in a park, although there was the occasional arrival from Italy of a black-rimmed envelope that never failed to sadden my parents.

Yes, I had questions and I turned to my brother Lou for the answers. He was only five years older than I, but he was my big brother and he knew everything. He explained that God had come calling and had taken Tonio away to Heaven. I countered that if God came for *me* I would run away. The response was that God was everywhere and that I could not run away from Him. Desperately, I came back with, "Well, I'll hide behind Mom and Pop!". And this, dear Reader, was the extent and depth of my theology at that point in time. It was a first sign, however, of a religious awakening and a realization that there was something meaningful beyond the playground or my next ice cream cone. The years have come and gone since that early exchange with Lou, and I can say that since then, I have neither run away nor hidden from God.

Frankly, when it comes to religion and all matters spiritual, the inhabitants of this planet have certainly made a mess of things. There are those pesky questions which have persisted through the ages, with the pages of human history serving as testimony that we have only succeeded in complicating matters in the quest for answers. Who-what is God? Where is He? How do we honor and pay homage to Him? Whose is the right philosophy or path to the Almighty? Indeed, does God exist?

All in the name of God, we have unleashed a plethora of "true" religions, "chosen" people and "enlightened" pathways; Christianity, Judaism, Buddhism and Islam are but a few. To further muddy the waters, Christianity splintered into Catholic, Baptist, Presbyterian, Mormon and many more, while Judaism divided into Reformed, Conservative, Orthodox, Hasidic. A follower of Islam can be Sunni or Shiite, or whatever. Holy books? The Bible, Koran and Book of Mormon easily come to mind.

In His name there have been crusades, inquisitions and even "holy" wars (an oxymoron, if there ever was one). Some religions sing the praises of God with hymns and chants, while others forbid music. For several religions, proper respect is shown when women enter with proper head covering, while the men must remove their hats. Can you imagine a busy, ever-patient God scratching His divine head as He observes Catholics crossing themselves from left to right while those of the Greek or Russian Orthodox faith go from right to left? All in the name of God.

My parents were, at most, sporadic churchgoers who nevertheless observed and nurtured at home all the religious holidays and traditions of our Catholic faith. We children were dutifully baptized and received the appropriate sacraments of Mother Church. The names of saints and the Deity were sometimes heard around home, at times attached to other words to reprimand us children. We were hustled off to Holy Mass every Sunday and required to attend weekly religious instructions during those formative years. The catechism was important in establishing guidelines for keeping me on the straight road; so was that backhand slap in the face I received from Sister Francesca for misbehaving in catechism class.

**I saw God...and** *she* was a beautiful child, attired in an elaborate robe and tiara and richly adorned with rings, bracelets and necklaces. This was Kumari, the current of a long line of living Hindu Goddesses who, in compliance with ancient Hindu tradition and dogma, reigns but a few years before returning to an ordinary life among us mortals. At a very early age, a child is observed and scrutinized for signs of special talents and traits indicative of an extraordinary being. She will leave her family and spend her childhood in luxury, comfort and, I am sure, utter boredom. I stood with a gathering in the courtyard of her palace in the Nepalese capital of Katmandu, awaiting the appearance of the child god. And like a child, she stepped onto the balcony, looked about indifferently, glanced down at us for a moment, turned, and went inside.

I met God...in the squalor and human misery of the broken streets and neighborhoods of Calcutta, India. I made it my personal mission to search out Mother Theresa somewhere in the labyrinth of that city of four million. So bold, yes, but it was the opportunity of a lifetime and I would not let it slip away. I would try a visit to the mother-house headquarters.

The chances of finding the saintly lady at home were next to zero. Mother Teresa and the good Missionaries of Charity are established not only in India, but worldwide, as well. They labor among the suffering masses, distributing food and caring for their needs. They run orphanages and homes for the aged, homeless and the terminally ill. A young sister appeared and I simply asked if Mother Teresa could spare a few minutes for me. "One moment," she said and vanished. With her crushing workload, surely she would not come out to waste valuable time speaking with Bart Scalzi of Poughkeepsie, New York. Suddenly, like a ghost, Mother Teresa materialized by my side. She was small in stature, bent forward, with her eyes fixed downward. Here before me stood the very embodiment of Christian charity, sacrifice and love humbly making herself available to a nobody such as I. No trumpets, no heavenly choir preceded her appearance. She quietly awaited my request.

Inspired by this marvelous woman, I visited one of her orphanages where I volunteered, with some local volunteers and several Belgian visitors, to help feed the numerous beautiful children. These babies were orphaned, abandoned or brought to the gate by desperate mothers and turned over to the good sisters. At mealtimes, the little ones were placed in their seats along the walls where we spoon-fed them and then settled them onto their potties to do their business. So funny to see an ocean of smiling little faces looking up, with their little bottoms tucked into their pots. They were adorable and so in need of hugs and caring. While I stood holding a child in my arms, I felt tugging at my pants legs. I looked down to see two "crawlers" looking up, wanting to be held. Holding and caressing one little toddler, she rewarded my good will by peeing on my shirt. The Belgian tourists were there to adopt children, and even I entertained the thought of leaving Calcutta with a little one in tow. I would certainly surprise my Mom with a "grandchild" but, realistically, the process would have taken many months.

I felt God's presence….high in the rugged Andean mountains of Peru. The bus climbed 8000 feet up the mountainside and, when we emerged at the top, I beheld an extraordinary setting. Before me lay the ancient ruins of a vanished civilization, resting under broad blue skies and surrounded by mountain peaks and sheer drops on all sides. The total silence was awesome This was Macchu Picchu, the lost city of the Incas!

The history books tell us that in the 16th century the Spanish conquistadors invaded and colonized Peru, driving some of the Inca people into the mountains where they isolated themselves and established a thriving community. Then, mysteriously, the flourishing community was abandoned, leaving us the remains of stone houses, shops, marketplaces, and terraces. I was struck with the feeling that I was standing on an altar while the several peaks positioned around me assumed the appearance of solemn, hooded monks - especially at dusk.

I met God once more...and He was in the guise of a Jesuit missionary priest serving the Saint Xavier Jesuit mission in the Nepalese city of Katmandu. That was John Dalheimer and the year was 1983. He defied description, and I grope now to find the appropriate words to best describe this one-of-a-kind man. Was he a reverent, soft-spoken, modest and gentle servant of the Lord? He was not. Did he minister among his flock in his black Jesuit robes and serve them gracefully in thought, word and deed? No, not exactly so.

He was a big guy, semi-burly, quite energetic and sporting a big, full gray beard that earned him the title of *Father Christmas* among the children during the holidays. He wandered through the mission and in the Katmandu streets in open sandals and wrapped in a brightly-colored robe that did more justice to the world of Buddhism than to Catholicism. His personality filled the room with his loud, jovial, good nature and theatrics. He was a showman, not for the sake of performing but, in his own way, in the fulfillment of his vows as a Catholic priest. Yes, he was a showman, a performer, a jolly fellow who marched to his own drummer - and he was a saintly man. The good padre, far from his California birthplace, had happily found his niche there, high up in the towering Himalayan mountains. St. Xavier's ministered to the Nepalese children of Katmandu and to those of refugee families from across the border in Tibet. The kids truly loved the big guy. He presented them to me and later offered me the opportunity to teach a class in his open-tented classroom. I beheld a sea of fifty smiling, beautiful children seated politely before me, and I set about presenting an improvised lesson of numbers, expressions and greetings in English, plus a couple songs and some cartoons drawn on a wobbly blackboard. All the while, Father John sat in the back with a broad grin on his bearded face.

He showed me a Nepalese-Tibetan prayer wheel and introduced me to *chang,* a popular local rice wine. For Sunday Mass I was invited to his humble quarters where I found him seated cross-legged on the floor, dressed in his Buddhist-style robe before a small platform that served as an altar. Totally focused on the celebration of the Mass, he was oblivious to my presence as he pursued his priestly duties. The religious community of St. Xavier was an interesting collection made up of a local priest, a Canadian priest (former Canadian Royal Mounted Policeman), an Indian padre, an American writer and Father John. There was even a visiting Protestant missionary in attendance. They shared a frontier spirituality. One evening, after a humble dinner of rice, greens and some sort of meat, Father John and I settled in his quarters for some chat and *chang*. I had questions about his life, his beliefs and the calling that brought him to missionary work in Asia. Jesuits are, of course, members of a religious order called The Society of Jesus, but I was not prepared for what followed when I probed further regarding his vocation and service. "I don't give a damn about anything else, not Mary, the saints, the Pope! I love and serve my Lord Jesus Christ - all else is secondary!" He was unequivocally blunt, serious and passionate in his faith. Period!

Father John was happily entrenched and resigned to spending his allotted years in God's service in this remote nowhere. Ultimately, he was to be denied that long stay. I remember his letter informing me that he had contracted a mysterious illness and would be uprooted and transferred back to the Jesuit community in Chicago. Father John was seriously ill and in urgent need of treatment. He opened the letter with, "Greetings from the lofty peaks and almighty spirit of the Kangri" and then went on to inform me of his diagnosis - but not in serious, heavy words. Rather, ever the performer, he spoke in delightfully playful and irreverent terms, informing me of "frizzy, wiggly creatures" that had emerged in his urine. One day, he left us and I was profoundly saddened. I envisioned a scenario where a smiling Father John, wearing his Buddhist robe, sandals and fluffy beard and with a cup of chang in his hand, approached those pearly gates and was received with a joyful, standing round of applause!

Has anyone seen God? The question can be answered with an emphatic "yes", for everyone has beheld His presence in His creation, in the lofty majesty of a mountain range, on the vast expanses of the deep sea. He is our good neighbor, that caring teacher and an ailing family member. Then I consider how over the years I have traveled and seen the reminders and markers of how we have sailed rudderless through history and dealt with our differences in destructive ways. There are military cemeteries in France, Italy and Belgium and others scattered elsewhere, all attesting to the fact that we have learned little or nothing. We continue with wars, discord and disorder. When not at war we shuffle papers at world conferences and deliver tired speeches about peace and harmony.

I imagine St. Francis of Assisi stepping up to the podium and, standing before a special session of the United Nations General Assembly, delivering his prayer for peace:

> Lord. Make me an instrument of your peace.
> Where there is hatred, let me sow love,
> Where there is injury, pardon,
> Where there is doubt, faith,
> Where there is despair, hope,
> Where there is darkness, light,
> Where there is sadness, joy.
>
> O divine Master, grant that I may not so much seek
> To be consoled as to console,
> To be understood as to understand,
> To be loved as to love.
> For it is in giving that we receive,
> It is in pardoning that we are pardoned,
> And it is in dying that we are born to eternal life.

# And the walls came tumbling down!

Democracy will leave Communism
in the dust bin of history.
-President Ronald Reagan (1911-2004)

*Traiasca Romania Libera!*

The poet Ralph Waldo Emerson memorialized in a few words the historic moment when a colonial people rose and united to proclaim its independence from a foreign master. He wrote of "The shot heard round the world" which launched the American Revolution and the birth of a new nation.

In 1989, a cry of freedom and new hope resounded throughout the world when the shackles of millions of enslaved peoples were shattered and cast aside. Soviet Communism was collapsing and Poland, Hungary, Czechoslovakia, Bulgaria, the Baltic countries and Russia itself were emerging from their horrific nightmare.

Long-suffering Romania, too, finally exploded out of its dreadful torment. I made my return in 1990, anxious to see a newly transformed land and its people relishing the fruits of newly-found liberty. It was but a year following the heroic revolution, and the reminders of that bloody struggle were evident throughout central Bucharest. Bullet holes adorned the walls of buildings, many streets and structures were broken, makeshift memorials for the fallen dotted the streets and squares; everywhere, the Romanian flag flapped in the breeze, proudly displaying a gaping hole in its center - a hole where once the odious Communist star had been.

The revolution in Romania ignited in the north where coalminers rose in protest and then hit Bucharest with a fury. The Securitate, the feared security forces, resisted fiercely until the army shifted and sided with the freedom fighters, turning the tide against the totalitarian oppressor. Nicolae Ceausescu, speaking from a balcony in Victoriae Square and delivering what was to be his last address to the masses, was met with shouts of defiance from the crowd, unheard of under that rigid regime. News footage shows a startled, unbelieving expression on his face. He withdrew and managed to escape by helicopter, but not for long. He was captured, quickly tried and, together with his wife Elena, shot on Christmas Day.

My return to post-revolutionary Romania was premature, for the country was struggling to get on its feet, and its economic transformation was yet to be realized. I looked for signs of progress and recovery and, indeed, there were new shops scattered about; entering a small market I quietly rejoiced when I saw not the barren shelves of past times, but real, honest-to-goodness merchandise aplenty. A new hotel or two had sprouted on Magheru Boulevard, evidence of new interest and investment from abroad. New construction was underway and beginning to give Bucharest a sorely needed facelift.

I *was* truly witnessing a transformation that went well beyond the physical and material well-being of a liberated people. The doors that opened had brought forth the intoxicating freshness and joy of freedom of the body, heart and mind of so many good people.

Although the ravages of oppression and deprivation were still to be erased, the new spirituality was manifest wherever I turned. A group of youngsters in a park strummed guitars and happily sang their popular tunes. People comfortably chatted, smiled and laughed in the new cafes that had appeared. The air seemed so sweet and fresh; the oppressive fog had dissipated.

Sentimentally and personally, I was visiting a new, free Romania, but one now become a shell for me, devoid of the soul that was my relationship with my Romanian friends. I was left with an emptiness and memories of years gone by. Wandering about, I passed the Carpati tourist office at the railway station where I first met Ortanza. Going by the hospital on Boulevard Magheru, I recalled how, as Doctor Scalzi, I "assisted" Serban in the operating room. There were several restaurants and beer gardens where my friends and I sometimes gathered to socialize or lament the plight of captive Romania.

A few years earlier, Ortanza finally ended her nightmare and left behind her painful existence under Communist rule. From the first day we met, I saw a suffering, angry and defiant rebel who fought the system head-on and succeeded only in creating more anguish and grief. Many of her wounds were self-inflicted because she refused to accept her fate and that made her more of a target of the authorities. How she longed to escape and fly off into free, blue skies! Fortunately, Ortanza met and married an Italian employee of Alitalia airlines and bid *la revedere* to her homeland forever. I do believe that it was a marriage of convenience, but it was her ticket to freedom.

As for Serban, his strategy of patient planning, preparation and cal-culation had paid off because he, too, had fled his captive homeland and established himself as a doctor-surgeon in the German city of Regensberg. How did he manage that? Incredibly, while biding his time in Romania he had taken his Romanian language medical books and transferred every-thing into the German language. He had retrained himself so well that he easily assumed his new status as a German citizen and professional. Serban was soon joined by his wife Adriana and their two sweet daughters, Ioana and Micaela.

There was one remaining link to the past which I needed to address. Sadly, Serban's dad had passed a few years before my return to Bucharest, but Mrs. Moldor was still alive and living in Brasov. I very much longed to visit her and embrace her once more. I wanted to comfort her in her declining years, but also to stir some fond memories of times gone by. With gifts for her, I hopped the train for a trip to Brasov. I approached the apartment building with happy anticipation and knocked at her door. There was no response and I turned to a neighbor and inquired in my fractured Romanian-French. She informed me that Maria Moldor had passed away but two months before. With a heavy heart, I returned to the railway station and boarded my train back. Before leaving Bucharest forever, I entered an Orthodox church and lighted candles in memory of dear Nicolae and Maria Moldor, two precious people.

I did see my dear friends Ortanza and Serban again. Ortanza and her Italian husband had established themselves in a comfortable apartment in Ostia, not far from central Rome. I was so anxious to see her again and to hear about her new life as a free woman. What were her first impressions? How had she adapted? How did she look? Had she finally found happiness? When she answered the door, I saw before me a smiling, exuberant woman, lovely as before and a bit more plump. That mask of sorrow and hopelessness had vanished. We had so much to talk about and, after a delicious dinner (she had mastered the Italian cuisine), her husband graciously left us to talk and get caught-up. She related that when she came to live in Rome, she marveled at the abundance of quality meat and seafood, the luscious fruit and crowded cafes and restaurants. It did not surprise me that she had become fluent in the Italian language. She certainly did possess an electronic brain, as she had once said to me.

Ortanza conducted a personal crusade against many of her neighbors who were, proudly, Italian Communists. At the time, Italy had the largest Communist party outside of Russia and it foolishly trumpeted the glories and well-being of world Communism. They messed with the wrong person! She was a spitfire and turned on those neighbors with a fury and passion as she related her own personal suffering and struggle under that tyrannical philosophy. A few years passed and I learned that Ortanza had separated from her husband and then, effectively, vanished off the radar screen.

And what of Serban? I had the good fortune of visiting the Moldor family in Regensburg on several happy occasions. Adriana was slowly and painstakingly learning German to qualify as a doctor in her new environment. The girls quickly assimilated and thrived in their new homeland, becoming fluent in German and English. One visit was particularly memorable. I did some grocery shopping in a local market and brought home the ingredients for an Italian dinner for my friends. It brought me back to that visit to Brasov when I fixed a similar dinner for Serban's mom and dad some years back. We enjoyed a happy meal together and the lively conversation about old Romania and their new-found fortunes.

I received word one sad day that Serban had suddenly and unexpectedly passed away, closing another door. Today, I maintain contact with the family which is prospering in Germany. Ioana is a lawyer, married and raising two children in Munich, while Micaela is a dental hygienist, married, and with two children, living in Wurzburg. I care deeply for these young people because of who they are and for what we shared in those troubled years gone by. I reserve a special place in my heart for my dear friends Ortanza and Serban. I thank them for their beautiful friendship and for the unforgettable role they played in my Romanian experience.

# Blattaphobia

A rose by any other name
Is still a rose.
-William Shakespeare (1564-1616)

*Et tu, Roachilius Uglius!*

No problem relating to that image of a woman standing on a chair and shrieking hysterically at the sight of a mouse; an ugly cockroach would cause a similar reaction on my part. And this is not insignificant because this phobia has qualified my travels throughout the years and continues to haunt them to the present day.

With apologies to Shakespeare – a roach by any other name is still a roach. If I book a room in Dusseldorf I will most certainly look out for a *kuchenschabe*. When I enter a room in Beijng and turn on the light, I pray no *zhanglang* makes an appearance. Whether a *cafarde* in Marseille, a *karaluch* in Warsaw, a *kackerlacka* in Stockholm, a *cucaracha* in Buenos Aires or a *blatta* in Venice, I loathe the little bastards! And they are not always little! I will not be visiting Madagascar anytime soon -I'm told that they have large *hissing* roaches scurrying about the terrain (shudder)!

The origin of this pathological aversion to the beasties can be traced to my earliest days of boyhood when my parents were making an issue of exterminating them wherever encountered in several homes we occupied in White Plains and Poughkeepsie. Out came the sprays, powders, boiling water...and the curses. Going to the bathroom at bedtime, turning on the light and seeing several of the monsters shooting for cover was enough to insure a sleepless night.

Serving on my first ship, USS Seneca operating out of Norfolk, Virginia, I got to know wonderful young guys from many parts of the country, but I also met some "shipmates" of the species *Roachilius Uglius* and I was not a happy sailor. One morning, I dragged myself into the mess hall and settled down for breakfast. Bleary-eyed and half asleep, I prepared to plunge into a bowl of cereal when I noticed that some of the raisins had legs. I grabbed a piece of toast and went forth to face the duties of the day. It was not unusual to open my locker and see a creature or two bolting for safety. I expected that one day on my way to a shower I might open the locker door and be greeted by a king -sized specimen handing me a towel.

Soon after Navy days, I launched my own personal travel career. The mere mention of the word *India* for me conjured up images of the exotic, adventurous and mysterious. In the summer of 1979, my British Air flight deposited me in the New Delhi airport for what was my introduction to the Orient. I checked into a rather nondescript hotel and then set out to explore the sprawling metropolis that lay before me. It was upsetting and incomprehensible to see, for the first time in my life, such squalor and human misery wherever I wandered.

That geography book back in grade school displayed photos of temples, veiled women wearing "dots" on their foreheads, and sacred cows wandering about the streets. It was all true. Strolling along a crowded Bombay street, a large animal came ambling out of a shop as casually as if it were crossing a green pasture. On another occasion, a ride on a city bus was abruptly halted by a "sacred" cow that had wandered into the center of the street and plopped down there. We dutifully and patiently waited until Blessed Bessy chose to move along in search of a shadier spot.

Returning to my room with a head full of wondrous sights and impressions, I prepared for a refreshing shower and a good night's rest. The room was creepy-looking, worn and gloomy with the added bonus of a dark, dank bathroom. Oh, my! Clean and revived, I settled down to write a few postcards, but only after doing some pushups. I hit the floor and pumped away until I looked up from my prone position and sighted across the room, at eye level, a big one that had emerged from the bathroom and paused there motionless. I did not wait to determine whether it was about to do pushups or launch an attack. I was airborne, landing on the safer heights of my bed from which vantage point I could observe the movements of my non-paying roommate. Sleepless night.

It was in 1981 that I discovered Nepal, a little monarchy tucked away in the shadow of Mt. Everest high in the Himalayas. This was a land of brightly-robed Buddhist monks, numerous temples, colorful marketplaces, stunning views and friendly people. There was talk of a living goddess in residence not far from Durbar Square. That enigma, Tibet, was nearby, just across the mountains. There were also Himalayan-grown roaches. Curses, I thought - they are all over creation!

The Woodhaven Hotel was centrally located in the Nepalese capital of Katmandu and it was a find! The very reasonable price provided me with a charming, comfortable room, nicely furnished and carpeted. A knock at the door and a young hotel worker appeared with a spray gun in his hand. Did I want my room sprayed? I politely declined, he shrugged his shoulders and departed. Probably some sort of exotic air freshener. I was unpacking and arranging when I spotted two objects lurking in a corner of the room. They were brownish and cigar-shaped, and with legs. From the Himalayan peaks of my bed I kept vigil throughout the night except for a few moments of dozing off. The next morning, stepping into the hallway to vacate the room and hotel, I beheld in the sunlight of the long corridor a parade of the creatures moving on the rug - revolting! If I had seen a corridor overrun by vipers I could not have been more horrified!

Curiously, even a phobia or a worst fear can take on a different aspect when one puts matters into perspective or finds the circumstances different. After harrowing episodes involving jumbo-sized cockroaches,

I developed a degree, albeit small, of tolerance for the specimens of more reasonable dimensions (I can't believe I said that!). I was rather hungry one day and wandered off the hot, dusty streets of Cairo and into a crowded, noisy eatery that normally I would have shunned by crossing the street to avoid its grubby, smelly atmosphere. However, I repeat, I was quite hungry. Looking over the stained menu I could not find any recognizable or identifiable edibles. The meat looked menacing and the platters at nearby tables were a showcase of grease, bad odors and disgusting colors. Reluctantly, I settled for a simple salad of tomatoes and greens with other "bits and pieces." After all, what could go wrong with a simple salad?

Poised to dig into my meal, I spotted a small roach that had climbed to the top of the salad and settled atop a chunk of lettuce. I never dreamed that I would react as I did, for I cocked my index finger, fired away and sent the creepy thing flying over to a nearby table. Then I ate the salad! I was hungry!

And then there was the battle that shook the world, at least the world that consisted of the four walls of The Fragrant Harbour Hotel in Hong Kong. It would prove to be my finest and defining moment in the struggle between good and evil. What unfolded behind the closed doors of my hotel room was a private war waged on a hot and humid summer evening. Following a refreshing shower, I settled down for several hours of relaxation watching local TV and browsing through the pages of the International Herald Tribune, my travel companion of many years. Having removed my glasses to focus better on my reading, I glanced off the page and spotted a dark, blurry object in a corner of the room. With my eyes fixed on the blur, I groped for my glasses, slipped them on, only to confirm my worst fears. What came into focus was a gargantuan cockroach! God! There goes my evening, my peace of mind, my emotional equilibrium. Tomorrow I will certainly pack my chopsticks and vacate the premises. But, that would be tomorrow. "What do I do now?" With nowhere to run, I made up my mind to stand my ground and fight! What I needed was to devise a solid strategy and to muster up the courage to do battle and slay the dragon.

With one eye on the invader-beast, the other swept the room surveying the battlefield. I spotted the thick Hong Kong telephone directory by the TV. Armed and ready, I cautiously maneuvered toward the target, extended my arms and, carefully aiming the projectile, prepared to fire. The plan was to have it fall accurately, flatten the cursed zhanglang and leave it covered until my escape the following morning. As I had no stomach for squashing sounds, precision was paramount and the thud and the size of the phonebook would adequately block out the sight and sound show resulting from the bombardment. The cockroach was tucked in close to the baseboard and made for a difficult target; there was little time to fret and wonder.

Bombs away! The book crashed to the floor with the desired thud - and missed! Oh, God! It missed! The roach scurried away (shudder) in the disgusting way roaches scurry and I took up a defensive position in the bathroom. I had suffered a setback in the very first phase of the battle and I bemoaned my misfortune. I retreated into the bedroom to rethink my military options and then return to the battlefield with renewed resolve and determination. What would Napoleon have done? Perhaps a flank maneuver or feign an attack to the left and then strike from the right. The monster was poised by a fixture under the sink, surely to make its escape into God knows what hidden niches of *my* room. What to do? I refused to squash the bug with a shoe for the reason previously mentioned.

Voila'- an idea! I moved to the sink and poured forth a big glass of scalding-hot water, I aimed carefully and poured the contents over the enemy. It was stunned and it squirmed (Ugh!) and staggered. I reloaded and fired away with another hot blast. That did it. It was still alive but immobilized. I felt as if I had knocked a tank out of action and that victory was finally at hand. I closed my eyes, clenched my teeth and sent it to roach heaven with the smack of a rolled-up magazine.. Then, looking away, I used a page of the magazine to scoop up the fallen warrior and gave it a military send-off by sliding it into the toilet bowl, flushing and sending it on its way out and into Hong Kong harbor. As I performed the ritual I recall triumphantly calling out, "1 won! Farewell, you *miserable* bastard!" In all the annals of warfare and military strategy, one will not find a single word written about this memorable battle waged in Hong Kong in the year 1980.

During my career teaching the Spanish language, I incorporated lessons in Spanish history and culture, including dancing Latin dances such as tango, rhumba, cha-cha and merengue. How ironic that I also taught the youngsters to sing and dance to an old, popular Mexican melody called... are you ready for this? "La Cucaracha!"

# Dear Mou...

Con te partiro'
-Andrea Bocelli

Happy anniversary! We celebrate the 20th year of a remarkable journey that we have happily shared and savored of the *joie de vivre* that life offers. Twenty years...can you believe it?

We might have honored the occasion by having lunch at the Brass Anchor Restaurant overlooking the Hudson River, as we did two decades ago on a lovely August afternoon. Unfortunately, that eating establishment no longer exists and we have celebrated instead with a glorious cruise to Alaska, a veritable jewel in the crown of USA. The scenery was spectacular everywhere we turned, and many misconceptions of our 49th state fell by the wayside as the days unfolded. It was a refreshing surprise to discover that Alaska is not a drab, cold iceberg tucked away in a remote corner of the map. We enjoyed soaking up twenty days of golden sunshine, blue skies and lovely flowers? Of course, you were in a photographer's paradise and you certainly snapped away to your heart's content, rivaling the chirping and tweeting of birds with the melodious click, click, click of your formidable camera.

Oh, I remember well one negative of our otherwise flawless trip. Thank God for aquariums and zoos and their wondrous bounty because some of God's creatures never made an appearance for us in the Wild. We did not ask to kiss a moose; we only wanted to see one in its natural habitat. No, we never got a chance. As for the grizzly, polar and brown bear so abundant in the Wild, they must have departed for another snooze in hibernation. Jokingly, I tried to ease the disappointment by commenting that the only way I would see a bear would be in the shower. You were not amused. The closest we came to a bear was having dinner at a Fairbanks restaurant called *Orso* and that is the Italian word for...*bear.*

Before we came together, Mou, I had already packed in a full and satisfying life of world travel and I could have simply "rested on my laurels" and coasted the rest of the way. I chose instead to continue my solo "bumming" across the continents, seeking new thrills and challenges. It had been fun making decisions and plans and then living with the consequences..

But then it happened. You came strutting into the hallowed halls of the sanctuary of my bachelorhood. Yes, you did! You trespassed where no other fair maid had ever trodden. So audacious, so invasive......so wonderful!

Friends have asked why I call you Mou and I explain that it is a term of endearment derived from the Greek and I use it as an ending to form *Lindakimou* or *My dear Linda*. I enjoy having a little fun affectionately applying nicknames tailored to fit the locales we have visited. You remember, traveling in South America you were *Gringuita* (from *Gringo),* while in China you became *Lin-Lin, Lindisima* in Spain, *Katrina* in Holland (because of your Dutch roots) and, when visiting sister Rosemarie and Jerry upstate in the Adirondacks region of New York State, you are my country girl, *Lindy Lou.*

Funny how we gradually came together. We were both Poughkeepsie language teachers and maintained a relationship on a professional level only, exchanging an occasional polite smile or greeting at a language department meeting. We talked briefly at one of those teacher Christmas parties, but then drifted away in different directions, although I recall walking away and thinking, "What a looker!" I dismissed any fantasies or illusions of ever walking off together with you, hand- in-hand and into the sunset.

I was wrong - happily wrong. It was pre-ordained that we should meet again and we did so one summer afternoon, in a most romantic setting: a local supermarket. It was my big chance! I conveniently remembered that I was composing a letter in poor French, addressed to the mayor of Valberg, a small village in the French Alps. It needed a French overhaul and *Voila*'! - you just happened to be a teacher of French, par *excellence*. Do you remember my story, Mou? Many years earlier, USS Marias made a stop at the French port of Cannes where several of us shipmates went off on a tour into the Alpine peaks. A group of bubbly, chattering Valberg children gathered to pose for a photo with me. I held a sweet little girl on my lap while the others around me waved, saluted and clowned for the camera. Years passed and when I came across the photo again, I made a decision to send it to the mayor and have it posted or circulated with the hope that some of the children might be identified or recognized and copies made for their families. To think, that today those darling little children would be grandparents!

Well, the rest is *histoire*. Our journey together was launched when we met at that cozy restaurant for a lunch that was to last until dinnertime. Finally, we were getting to know each other. Our origins, we learned, were similar in that we shared poor and humble backgrounds...I, in White Plains, New York and you, in Pottersville, in northern New York. But, compared with you, I was a prince living in a storybook castle, while your family managed in a refurbished garage with cold concrete floors and without indoor running water or toilet. On a visit upstate, you took me to see the old garage for myself. Oh, my, Mou!

Our paths, however, diverge somewhat. You loved school and have often said how much you admired and revered your teachers. Yes, I know that you are a bit uncomfortable when I tell others that you were the class valedictorian at Pottersville High School, although it was a graduating class of only 12 students. You were later crowned valedictorian at New York State University at New Paltz, in a class of over 2000 graduates! Brava!

Meanwhile, I was a rudderless, aimless young guy plodding along without a goal or purpose in life until, fortunately, I was rescued by the US Navy.

Overall, our travel *modus operandi* is right on track, but with some differences when it comes to our "travel personalities". You are, unquestionably, Miss Intensity/Go-getter and I, Mr. Laid-back/Kid Casual. Other words may help to paint the picture: you happily *gulp* the world about us while I quietly *savor,* you joyfully *swallow* all the wonders of art, nature and architecture and I *nibble,* you *slurp* deliciously while I *sip* deliberately, It is often *quantity* as opposed to *quality.* Perhaps I can summarize it best this way: visiting a lovely Japanese garden is a delightful treat, but if there are ten Japanese gardens in Tokyo, you would want to visit eleven. As a consequence, we agree that occasionally I will sit out a museum and choose to luxuriate at a nearby cafe, sipping a *cafe au lait* and watching the world go by while, inside, you enjoy treasured moments in the hallowed company of Rembrandt, Caravaggio, Vermeer, Leonardo, Renoir and El Greco. Everybody's happy!

When it comes to photography, you once told me that you wore out a camera taking a billion photos. You do indeed snap everything: flowers, mountains, sunsets, architecture, birds, babies; nary a gnat escapes your feverish appetite and wicked clicking finger. Ah, but the photos you take. Your work is beautifully done and the DVDs which you have meticulously and artistically produced have entertained many friends at our parties. On the other hand, I no longer own a camera. I took photos years ago, but it all wore off. It's likely that your photographic wizardry has put me out of business.

You recall the luggage issue on those early trips? I traveled with a small carry-on while you felt it necessary to bring along "La Bestia" and a beast of a bag it was! But, Dear Mou, did you have to burden me with *two* of them? I know I was young and strong, thank you, but I was not King Kong. Ultimately, we found some solutions: No longer pack clothes for every day of a month's trip, bring along some detergent for a little room laundry, use the hotel laundry service, if available, or visit a laundromat. And I found a practical solution for the tablecloth issue. In our quest for a meal we have come upon a quaint brasserie in Paris or discovered a charming ristorante in Venice and we checked it out. We peek through the window and, if there are no tablecloths on the tables, you give it a thumbs down and we move on. One could get very hungry doing this. Tell me what you think of this: for our next trip...pack a tablecloth. Period! But I will positively, absolutely refuse to help you set the table at a restaurant. I also offer a solution for your annoyance at not finding a hook on a bathroom door; we can pack a hook and screwdriver and install it from hotel to hotel, as needed – or maybe not.

And politics? That most toxic and incendiary of subjects!? We are both aware that political discourse today can easily morph into political discord with unpleasant consequences. Families fracture, friendships crumble, and lawyers, psychiatrists and therapists make money. You and I have the perfect solution - we avoid it like the bubonic plague! However, when traveling, we quietly display our political identity at the bathroom towel rack: my towel is on the right and yours on the left. Such creative geniuses!

We are, however, on the same page in so many things. We do enjoy ballroom dancing and can really hold our own with a mean tango, a graceful waltz or a peppery cha-cha. Our rhythmic rumba is not bad, either. We certainly enjoyed dancing a tango when we came across a street musician playing in that Paris metro. We love opera; your favorite being Puccini's *Turandot,* with that magnificent aria *Nessun dorma*. Mine is Pietro Mascagni's *Cavalleria Rusticana,* a one-act gem. How delightful was that puppet presentation of Mozart's *The Magic Flute* in Germany!

There have been other occasions when you have soared to the pinnacle of my admiration. You may pooh-pooh the story, but I was so proud of you. It was on that two-week visit we made to Washington D.C. a few years back. We were visiting Ford's Theater, where our favorite president was shot in 1865. On the lower level there is an excellent Lincoln museum where I was busy browsing along a wall display when I heard a loud, angry voice behind me shouting, "How dare you!" I turned and saw that it was you, Linda, and repeating, "How *dare* you?" You managed to explain to me that you had witnessed a boy of about ten approach a statue of Abraham Lincoln, reach up and slap his face several times. "How dare you disrespect this great man!" The mother of the boy explained that he was just a young boy, but that only angered you further and you gave her a lesson, as well, telling her that her son was old enough to learn not to dishonor a beloved American icon. You were angry, you were indignant - you were marvelous!

Yes, we've taken some lumps along the way, as well. We both had close calls while on the road, experiences that not only could have blotted out a trip, but also our very lives. In September of 2012, you assumed the role of my personal guardian angel and your performance was stellar! St.Vincent Hospital's excellent care in treating my skull and spinal fractures and doing needed surgery is only half the story. During those two weeks of hospitalization, you consulted with the medical team on my behalf and kept me informed all the way. You made many calls to USA and informed my family. Your communication with the insurance company was of incalculable value and ultimately resulted in total coverage of medical expenses and our first-class flight home. To think that I had pooh-poohed taking out travel insurance. Never used it before – because I was indestructible – until I got "destructed" in Sydney. You insisted on it, saving me over $100,000 in medical bills and flights home. I insisted that you spend each day exploring Sydney while I was in St. Vincent's and you took care of yourself quite well. When you visited me with an ice cream each day, I heard of your enjoyable discoveries and activities across the city. Mou, sometimes I reflect back to that near-tragic day and think that we flew happily together to Australia, but you nearly ended up flying home alone – and accompanying a body!

Our adventure in Peru was one of the most memorable in all our travels together. It was the land of the Incas and they certainly had left their indelible mark in the music, ruins and faces of that exotic land. There were the native llamas, alpacas and vicuna, distinct Inca culture, and - there was altitude sickness. That was an unhappy experience that befell you in the city of Cuzco. The local inhabitants and the llama went about their daily business at an altitude of 11,152 feet, a bit much for unfortunate aliens such as we.

I was chatting in the hallway with two other travelers when I noticed several hotel people running down the hallway carrying oxygen equipment. What really alarmed me was seeing them turn into our room! I burst in and found you sobbing and gasping on the bed as the staff prepared the oxygen. "I want to go home," you said between sobs. On the very next day, you followed up your ordeal with an astoundingly unexpected feat. Feeling like Wonder Woman once more, you wanted to climb to the pinnacle of Huayna Picchu which was, at 8,920 feet, much higher than nearby Macchu Picchu. I thought that the lack of oxygen had muddled your mind. Well, we scaled that almost vertical, precarious trail. The view from the top, looking down on Macchu Picchu, was truly stunning!

We have covered a lot of terrain and shared so many memorable moments. We both appreciate the diversity of the cultures we encounter and we simply wallow in the fun of employing our language skills wherever we go. Isn't it fun using our Spanish, Italian and French? I like our practice of learning some rudimentary language of the country we are visiting; we did this for trips to Japan, Russia and China. I am sure that we must sound like "Hollywood Indian talk" but we do communicate and have a jolly good time doing it.

This closing chapter of my autobio-travelogue certainly does not rise to the heights and grandeur of the Holy Bible, the U.S. Constitution or the Emancipation Proclamation but, nevertheless, my words and sentiments pour forth from my heart as a loving tribute to a caring life's companion and wonderful travel mate. Together, we have marveled at Mother Nature's Grand Canyon masterpiece and that glorious sunset in the sculptured landscape of Utah and the big blue skies of the Australian Outback.. You and I have walked the Great Wall and hiked in the Andean mountains. We have been dazzled by the uniqueness of Australian wildlife and stood in awe before the presidents at Mt. Rushmore. We have loved and have been loved by dear family and friends here and abroad. We have been abundantly blessed with these twenty rich years of treasured remembrances, and we are so grateful to God. I very much hope that I have been a good mate for you as you have been for me and that I have left you with no regrets.

That said, grab your passport, Mou. Place your hand in mine and let's get out of here. We've got a flight to catch.

Made in the USA
Las Vegas, NV
10 August 2022